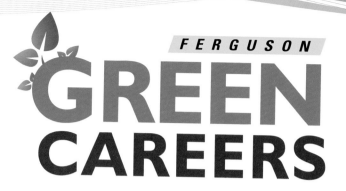

LAW, GOVERNMENT & PUBLIC SAFETY

FERGUSON

GREEN
CAREERS

LAW, GOVERNMENT
& PUBLIC SAFETY

PAMELA FEHL

Ferguson Publishing
An imprint of Infobase Publishing

Ferguson
An imprint of Infobase Publishing
132 West 31st Street
New York NY 10001

Library of Congress Cataloging-in-Publication Data
Fehl, Pamela.
  Law, government, and public safety / Pamela Fehl.
    p. cm. — (Green careers)
  Includes bibliographical references and index.
  ISBN-13: 978-0-8160-8152-3 (hardcover : alk. paper)
  ISBN-10: 0-8160-8152-2 (hardcover : alk. paper) 1. Environmental management—Vocational guidance—Juvenile literature. 2. Public lands—Protection—Vocational guidance—Juvenile literature. 3. Professional employees in government—Vocational guidance—Juvenile literature. 4. Environmental engineers—Juvenile literature. 5. Park rangers—Juvenile literature. 6. City managers—Juvenile literature. I. Title.
  GE60.F453 2010
  333.72—dc22   2009046019

Ferguson books are available at special discounts when purchased in bulk quantities for businesses, associations, institutions, or sales promotions. Please call our Special Sales Department in New York at (212) 967-8800 or (800) 322-8755.

You can find Ferguson on the World Wide Web at http://www.fergpubco.com

Text design by Annie O'Donnell
Composition by EJB Publishing Services
Cover printed by Bang Printing, Brainerd, MN
Book printed and bound by Bang Printing, Brainerd, MN
Date printed: April 2010
Printed in the United States of America

10 9 8 7 6 5 4 3 2 1

This book is printed on acid-free paper.

All links and Web addresses were checked and verified to be correct at the time of publication. Because of the dynamic nature of the Web, some addresses and links may have changed since publication and may no longer be valid.

Contents

Introduction

Environmental policies exist because individuals and groups identified the problems and recognized that standards and laws needed to be set, regulated, and enforced. The federal government established the Environmental Protection Agency (EPA) in 1970 to help protect the environment and public health. Environmental laws existed before this time, but it was the founding of the EPA, and the ensuing environmental movement in the 1970s, that inspired interest in improving the health of the planet. It has since sparked the enactment of numerous laws as well as countless amendments to older regulations.

Professions within the environmental law, government, and public safety field have also emerged and evolved due to stricter laws and in direct relation to the interests of the administrations in power. Whether protecting wildlife by policing and monitoring habitats; preserving lands by enacting and defending laws; ensuring human and environmental health by testing and assessing land, air, and water qualities; or even creating, renovating, and managing healthy communities and cities, the professionals who work in this field are rewarded with the knowledge that their efforts today contribute to improved life for future generations.

In this volume, you will find a variety of jobs to help you gain a better understanding of the areas of law, government, and public safety in which you can work. Keep in mind that what you see here is merely the tip of the iceberg: Plenty of other occupations and specializations exist within this group. The jobs covered here are meant to help you discover the environmental issues you are most passionate about, and allow you to see which type of work you can envision yourself eventually doing. Featured professions include city managers, conservation officers, environmental engineers, environmental health officers, environmental lawyers, environmental planners, environmental specialists, environmental technicians, EPA special agents (Criminal Investigation Division), fish and game wardens, hazardous waste management specialists, hazardous waste management technicians, land acquisition professionals, land trust or preserve managers, and park rangers.

The profiles are organized into 12 sections, so you can easily refer to specific aspects of each job, such as basic job descriptions, educational requirements, or salary summaries. You will also be able to determine if your personality and character line up with the job requirements.

- **Quick Facts** is exactly that—a fast look at job basics, such as salary range and future outlook for the career.
- **Overview** describes the job responsibilities in several short sentences.
- **History** tells you why the job began, and highlights landmark events and milestones within the industry.
- **The Job** provides you with specifics about the work, including the day-to-day tasks, the teams and people involved, and the project goals. You will note that some profiles include comments and insights from people working in the field.
- **Requirements** helps you map out courses you can start taking right now. It leads you from high school courses to post-graduate studies and beyond. **Other Requirements** gives you an idea of additional skills, talents, and personality traits needed to succeed in the job.
- **Exploring** gives you tips on ways to learn more about the job and the industry. You will find suggestions for reading materials, professional associations, and other resources in this section.
- **Employers** explains the types of industries and companies that hire the featured professional. This section may feature statistics about the number of professionals working in the United States, and the states and/or cities that pay higher salaries. Statistics are often derived from the U.S. Department of Labor (DoL), the National Association of Colleges and Employers, and professional industry-related associations.
- **Starting Out** offers you insights into how to get a foot in the door, and may explain the path some professionals take to secure entry-level jobs.
- **Advancement** shows the various ways to advance within the field.
- **Earnings** features salary information based on surveys conducted by the DoL, and sometimes from such employment specialists as Salary.com or PayScale.com.
- The **Work Environment** section describes the typical surroundings and conditions of employment. Also discussed are typical hours worked, any seasonal fluctuations, and the stresses and strains of the job.

❧ **Outlook** is not a crystal ball, but forecasts employment opportunities for the specific job and industry based on DoL surveys, professional associations' studies, or experts' insights on the field.

❧ **For More Information** ends the profile by providing you with even more resources, such as contact information for professional associations you may want to join, educational organizations that offer certification or workshops and conferences, and other resources you can use to learn more about the job.

As you read through each profile, be sure to take notes, keep track of your own independent research, and, most important of all, enjoy the process!

City Managers

OVERVIEW

City governments across the country vary in structure. Some may have a mayor-council, others may have a commission or a city manager. *City managers* are hired, paid administrators who work closely with the city council and mayor to manage the city. Their work usually involves supervising most of the city departments, writing budgets, enforcing policy, advising the city council on policies, and attending meetings and participating in press conferences.

HISTORY

Local government is usually structured in two ways—mayor-council or council-manager—and is sometimes structured with a combination of the two. Levels of authority will vary depending on the size of the city and the history of its government structure. In the mayor-council government, the mayor may play a strong role, having much of the administrative authority, with the council and public having some oversight. Many large cities, such as New York City, have this type of "strong-mayor" government. In smaller cities, the council may have strong administrative authority, with the mayor serving in a more ceremonial capacity.

In the council-manager type of government, the mayor chairs the council, and the number of members in the council depends on the city. The council appoints a city manager to administer the city's business and research and implement policy as needed. While the mayor and council members are elected officials, city managers are hired staff members who work at the discretion of the council.

The council-manager, or city-management, government came about in the early 20th century. Until then, the structure of many city governments was in dire need of a redesign. Political parties were at the helm, running the city according to their political interests and not the citizens', and corruption was viral. Mayors were often all-powerful and commonly referred to as "bosses," and for good reason. Employment in local government was based on patronage; and kickbacks from city contractors and vendors, as well as skimming on contracts, was rampant.

The city-management type of government was introduced in the early 1900s to combat the corruption and put control of the city into the hands of an objective, experienced business manager—an outsider who was hired to run the city similar to the way a business would be run. As described in the book *The Public Administration Theory Primer*, "Civil service systems replaced patronage. . . The election of city council members changed from districts to at-large. . . And an entirely new form of government was invented, a form based not on the separation of powers but on the corporate model." The city council, which could be likened to a company's board of directors, was small and consisted of volunteers who were devoted more to civic duty than to building political careers by whatever means possible. The day-to-day work was assigned to a city manager, tasked with ensuring that the city government ran efficiently and honestly.

In 1908 Staunton, Virginia, became the first city to have a city manager. And in 1912 Sumter, South Carolina, was the first city to adopt a charter incorporating the basic principles of city-management government. Today, almost half of all U.S. cities with populations of 2,500 or more have a city-management system of government, according to the International City/County Management Association.

THE JOB

Sometimes called *chief administrative officers*, city managers are appointed administrative managers of cities that have a council-manager or city-management system of government. They are

Steve Schainker, city manager of Ames, Iowa, addresses reporters in a news conference regarding possible contamination of the city's wastewater treatment system. *AP Photo/Ames Tribune, Nirmalendu Majumdar*

executive-level professionals who are hired by city councils to oversee all aspects of the daily operation of cities. Most city managers have at least 10 years of experience in public administration.

The city council and mayor define the city manager's job responsibilities. While the city manager can, and should, make suggestions for actions, the manager cannot take these actions on his or her own. City managers present their ideas to the city council for approval; only after approval is received can the ideas be implemented. Their job responsibilities are diverse, and include helping to get policy enacted within the city, hiring and managing staff, and developing and managing city services. City managers also direct and supervise city departments, such as finance, port and harbor, and parks and recreation.

In smaller cities city managers will have more responsibilities because staff support will be minimal. For example, the city of Edgewood, Washington—8.9 square miles, 9,615 residents—was seeking a city manager in September 2009. Its manager, reporting to the city council, serves as the chief executive officer of the city. In such a capacity, the job entails implementing policy as established by the city council, directing issues to the city council for its review and consideration, recommending policy options, and also conducting research and analysis when requested by the city council. Edgewood was seeking a professional "working manager," someone who could perform the job with limited administrative staff support.

A big part of a city manager's job is attending meetings. Managers are responsible for helping to guide the city in the right direction, so keeping up with the activities, interests, and issues of different groups and individuals, and providing information, resources, and input when needed are important components of the job. City managers attend city council meetings, department meetings, committee meetings, planning and commissions meetings, meetings with organizations and associations, meetings with citizens' groups and citizens, press meetings, and so on. They are involved in labor relations and contract negotiations, and attend business and community group meetings to hear what's on people's minds; they bring this information back to the city council to brainstorm solutions. They may help resolve conflicts and create new or improved partnerships. And then there are luncheons and dinners, and numerous special events that city managers are required to attend and participate in. They may also be required to prepare news releases to be distributed to the media as well as give interviews.

City managers seeking work in 2006 would have seen the following responsibilities included in the city manager job description posted by the city of Petaluma, California (whose population in 2006 was approximately 56,727):

- Direct the preparation and administration of the annual budget and capital projects for the city.
- Recommend legislation and policies required in the public interest.
- Coordinate the preparation of a wide variety of reports or presentations to the city council or outside agencies.
- Prepare and recommend long-range plans for city services and programs; develop specific proposals for action on current and future city needs.
- Enforce the provisions of public utility franchises, contracts, leases, and agreements; make final interpretations of city regulations and various ordinances, codes, and applicable laws to ensure compliance.

❉ Handle citizen appeals of lower-level administrative decisions.

❉ Direct the selection, supervision, and the work evaluation of departmental personnel; and direct citywide employee relations, staff development, and grievance procedures, including directing and participating in labor negotiations.

❉ Direct the development and implementation of management systems, procedures, and the application of standards for program evaluation on a citywide basis.

REQUIREMENTS

High School

A good basis for future work as a public service employee, such as city manager, includes course work in business, math, social science, history, English, computers, and a foreign language.

Postsecondary Training

Many cities, although not all, require city managers to have a master's degree. For some cities, an undergraduate degree in business administration, public administration, finance, or a related field will usually suffice. Course work in economics, statistics, sociology, statistics, urban planning, political science, finance, and management is beneficial.

Other Requirements

The job of city manager is demanding on multiple levels. People skills are required—a proven track record in successfully working with a variety of people with diverse backgrounds is essential. Strong communication skills—the ability to listen to residents, representatives from various groups, council members, and to clearly present ideas and solutions—are key to succeeding in the job. The hours are long, often extending into evenings and weekends. Flexibility and willingness to sacrifice personal time for civic duties are intrinsic to accomplishing city-management work.

Other requirements include extensive knowledge of federal, state, and local laws, regulations and policies; of current principles, practices, and techniques for evaluating the needs of the city; the ability to effectively communicate with the public; the ability to plan, manage, assign, and evaluate work of support staff; and the ability to evaluate socioeconomic and physical problems of city populations.

EXPLORING

Visit the Cities 101 section of the National League of Cities Web site (http://www.nlc.org/about_cities/cities101.aspx) for a full introduction to everything you might want to know about cities—from facts and statistics, to city charters and powers, city government structures, elections and elected officials, and city finances. You can also keep up with your city government and learn more about its structure and operations by regularly visiting your city's Web site. For example, New York City's Web site is NYC.gov (http://nyc.gov); the District of Columbia's Web site is DC.gov (http://www.dc.gov); and Seattle's Web site is Seattle.gov (http://www.seattle.gov). If you don't know your city's Web address, just use a search engine such as Google, plug in your city's name followed by the word "government," and the address should be among the first few entries that come up.

EMPLOYERS

Small and medium-sized cities, with populations ranging from 10,000 to 500,000, usually have a city-management government. City managers in small cities may have an administrative assistant to help them manage their schedules, field calls and emails, and handle other daily office tasks. In larger cities, city managers generally have more staff support, such as an assistant manager for each department.

STARTING OUT

One way that city managers gain experience is by working as management analysts or assistants in government departments that work with councils and mayors. They may also gain experience by moving to an executive position in a government agency or becoming a deputy or assistant city manager. While in college, an internship is the best way for students interested in this type of work to gain useful experience as well as college credit. Many graduate programs require students to participate in internships that range from six to 12 months in duration. Students can also gain practical experience by starting out as administrative assistants or other junior-level administrative positions in local government.

You can learn more about public administration and the role city managers play by reading such books as *City Management: Keys to Success*, by Orville W. Powell; and *The Public Administration Theory Primer*, by Kevin B. Smith, et al.

ADVANCEMENT

City managers who work for small cities can advance by taking city manager positions with larger cities. They may move on to other positions within city government. They may also take teaching positions in colleges and universities, or return to the private sector to work for corporations or start their own businesses.

EARNINGS

Salaries for city managers vary depending upon the size of the city, the region in which the city is located, the responsibilities of the city manager, and the level of experience. According to Payscale.com, in 2009 city managers with less than one year of experience earned median incomes ranging from $49,132 to $73,250. Those who had five to nine years of experience averaged $51,366 to $97,134 per year. City managers with 20 or more years of experience brought home $87,257 to $157,129.

California and Illinois were among the top-paying states for city managers, with California offering annual salaries ranging from $97,023 to $202,996 for its city managers, and Illinois paying median annual salaries ranging from $71,321 to $152,308.

In addition to salary, city managers also receive employment benefits such as health and life insurance, paid medical leave and personal days, vacations, and pension plans.

WORK ENVIRONMENT

City managers work long hours in offices as well as at other locations. They attend meetings, press conferences, luncheons, and dinners. They visit regularly with associations and organizations, and they also meet with citizens in various districts. This is not a 9-to-5 job, and it requires hard work, commitment, and mental and physical stamina. The ability to travel when needed and to work beyond business hours, into the evenings and weekends, is essential for success in this type of work.

OUTLOOK

The U.S. Department of Labor forecasts slower than average employment growth in state and local governments through 2016. Budget constraints and outsourcing of government jobs to the private sector may diminish opportunities for administrative and management positions with city governments. When the economy is stable and cities are able to add more money to their budgets, job seekers may find more employment opportunities. City manager jobs will be available as city budgets permit. Jobs will also open up as people retire or leave positions for other work.

FOR MORE INFORMATION

Learn more about careers in public service by visiting the ASPA's Web site.

American Society for Public Administration (ASPA)
1301 Pennsylvania Avenue, NW, Suite 840
Washington, DC 20004-1735
Tel: 202-393-7878
Email: info@aspanet.org
http://www.aspanet.org

Find news, conferences, meetings, events, and other resources by visiting

International City/County Management Association
777 North Capitol Street, NE, Suite 500
Washington, DC 20002-4201
Tel: 202-289-4262
http://www.icma.org

Find information about city trends and demographics, legislative and policy updates, and more, by visiting

National League of Cities
1301 Pennsylvania Avenue, NW, Suite 550
Washington, DC 20004-1747
Tel: 202-626-3000
Email: info@nlc.org
http://www.nlc.org

Conservation Officers

School Subjects
Biology
Earth science

Personal Skills
Helping/teaching
Leadership/management

Work Environment
Primarily outdoors
One or more locations

Minimum Education Level
Bachelor's degree

Salary Range
$29,656 to $42,107 to $91,000

Certification or Licensing
None available

Outlook
About as fast as the average

OVERVIEW

Conservation officers work to protect the natural resources of the local environment. They are specially trained officers who are licensed to carry firearms and to enforce federal and state environmental laws and regulations by conducting investigations of complaints, serving warrants, and making arrests. Their work also involves educating the general public about protecting the environment and about environmental laws.

HISTORY

Industrialization throughout the United States in the 19th century, coupled with rapid population growth and expansion of cities, caused great damage to the environment. Open spaces were being consumed, natural habitats were being destroyed, and animals were disappearing. The passenger pigeon, for instance, a bird that was at one time as common in North America as the sparrow is today, went from a population that some estimate to have been in the billions, to zero by the early 1900s. People hunted and ate the passenger pigeon out of existence.

The American bison nearly had a similar fate around the same time. Its near extinction is blamed on a combination of commercial hunting (for the bison's skin), the U.S. federal government's sanctioning of bison hunting (to weaken the Native American Indian population by removing its main food source), and overhunting by Native Americans (who were killing bison at a rate per year that was nearing the maximum of sustainability for that area). Land development was also disrupting bison herds and diminishing populations. At the turn of the 20th century, several ranchers started reintroducing bison to the North American population to prevent extinction. The Wildlife Conservation Society, founded in 1895, also helped restore the American bison on the Western Plains. Many ranches and conservation parks have bison herds residing on them today, but Yellowstone National Park is the only place in the country where a continuously wild bison herd can be found. Descended from 23 bison that had survived a massive hunt in the 1800s, the Yellowstone herd ranges in population from 3,000 to 3,500 bison.

On October 25, 1916, President Woodrow Wilson signed the act that created the National Park Service. Known as the Organic Act, the original goal, which still holds true today, was to "promote and regulate the use of Federal areas known as national parks, monuments and reservations . . . by such means and measures as conform to the fundamental purpose of the said parks, monuments and reservations, which purpose is to conserve the scenery and the natural and historic objects and the wild life therein and to provide for the enjoyment of the same in such manner and by such means as will leave them unimpaired for the enjoyment of future generations."

Since then, the conservation movement has evolved and grown. Books that heightened awareness about environmental issues included Aldo Leopold's *A Sand County Almanac*. Published in 1949, the book features essays by Leopold, an ecologist and environmentalist, about the land around his home in Sauk County, Wisconsin, his thoughts on conservation, and his ideas about having a "land ethic" and an "ecological conscience." Rachel Carson's *Silent Spring*, published in 1962, was another influential book in the conservation movement, shedding light on the dangers of pesticide use and the importance of being responsible, good stewards of the earth and wildlife.

The Environmental Protection Agency was created in 1970. Many environmental laws and regulations have been passed since then, including the Endangered Species Act, and numerous conservation groups, such as Worldwatch Institute, the Natural Resources

Defense Council, and Greenpeace, have since been established to help protect natural resources and wildlife on land and in water.

THE JOB

Conservation officers are tasked with enforcing environmental laws and regulations related to wildlife and fish, state parks and forests, trails, waters, and wetlands. They work for federal and state agencies, are rigorously trained at police academies, and are licensed to carry firearms. If a federal wildlife law has been broken, they are authorized to cross state lines to serve warrants and make arrests. The types of crimes they may deal with include violations of commercial fishing, trapping, and hunting laws; and snowmobiling and other activities in no-trespassing zones. When recreational accidents occur, conservation officers are usually among the first on the scene to investigate the circumstances.

Conservation officers are responsible for documenting state and federal misdemeanors, felonies, and other violations of environmental conservation laws. They research and investigate complaints regarding conservation law infractions, and strategize the plans for approach, interrogation, and, if needed, arrest. They process violators, collect and document evidence, and then write and submit reports. To ensure environmental compliance, they also conduct audits of commercial operations. Entry-level conservation officers usually report to an area supervisor, but they are expected to exercise independent judgment and take immediate actions when necessary.

Once they have completed their training, conservation officers are assigned to work in a specific area. Their day-to-day tasks will vary depending on the weather and terrain of the region. They may travel by car, boat, snowmobile, motorcycle, on foot, or even by airplane to observe people and make sure all activities, such as hunting, fishing, recreation, etc., are being done according to the conservation laws. They may check the licenses of hunters, anglers, and trappers, and inspect their equipment and the species being taken, to make sure they are in compliance. Conservation officers also inspect snowmobiles, all-terrain vehicles (ATVs), off-road vehicles, and watercraft to ensure the registration is correct and up to date, and to confirm the vehicles and equipment are being operated appropriately. They also enforce conservation laws and regulations regarding the use of forests and parks, such as making sure that trash, gas, and oil are properly disposed of. If a violation is evident, conservation officers are authorized to seize

A nature conservation officer inspects a pelican covered in oil from a cargo ship. *AP Photo/Tertius Pickard*

equipment, serve warrants for arrests, issue summons to appear in court, and make physical arrests of violators. They may also be required to appear in court to testify and provide evidence regarding the case.

Another aspect of the job entails communicating with the general public and the media. Conservation officers may work on public relations and outreach programs, as well as make presentations at schools and community and service group meetings to educate people about environmental conservation and laws. Some positions may require conservation officers to teach hunter and angler classes, in addition to courses in hunting and trapping, and safety courses for boating, snowmobiling, and ATVs. Conservation officers are also responsible for maintaining the equipment they use on the job, such as outboard motors, snowmobiles, and guns.

In addition to enforcement tasks, conservation officers are required to keep close tabs on the environment and wildlife in their assigned area. They take notes, collect data, and report their findings on the condition of fish and wildlife, and sightings of pollution. They investigate complaints about birds and animals that are causing problems, and consult with wildlife biologists to learn about possible reasons for the behavior and suggested solutions. Once a solution is decided upon, they educate the general public about techniques for controlling the problem animals.

Conservation officers work closely with state and federal enforcement agencies, including the state police, sheriff, and the U.S. Fish and Wildlife Service. When needed, they help search for missing persons and suspected criminals, manage roadblocks, and interview witnesses and suspects.

REQUIREMENTS
High School
Take as many science classes as possible—biology, earth science, environmental and conservation studies, geology, etc.—as well as math, history, English, computers, and foreign language. Conservation officers need to be physically fit to do their work, so be sure to take physical education classes and exercise regularly on your own.

Postsecondary Training
Many employers prefer job candidates to have a bachelor's degree, but an associate's degree along with work experience may be sufficient for some. The New York State Department of Environmental

Conservation, for example, requires a bachelor's degree, or an associate's degree coupled with either one year of work experience in freshwater or marine sciences, wildlife sciences, forestry, environmental engineering, or environmental technology; one year of police officer experience with Municipal Training Course certification; or two years of active U.S. military service with an honorable discharge. Course work in natural-resource conservation, environmental science, environmental studies, natural science, physical science, and criminal justice is useful in this field.

Other Requirements

Work hours vary and may be spent indoors for report writing, research, and teaching, and outdoors in any kind of weather for everything else required for the job. Physical fitness and mental stability are mandatory for the position, and physical fitness must be maintained throughout one's career in order to pass random fitness tests. Some positions may require conservation officers to know how to swim, cross-country ski, hike, and/or snowshoe. Conservation officers also need to know first aid, how to operate a chainsaw (e.g., to clear fallen trees and branches from paths), wilderness survival tactics, and map and compass skills (including GPS—global positioning system). Applicants for conservation officer positions must be U.S. citizens, at least 21 years old, and residents of the state in which they are applying for work. They must have a clean record, possess a valid driver's license, and be willing to undergo a thorough background investigation. Applicants must be people with upstanding moral character who are responsible, ethical citizens.

Training requirements for conservation officers vary by state. All officers must go through a training academy for a specified amount of time to become fully authorized conservation officers. For example, conservation officers for the New York State Department of Environmental Conservation (DEC) must complete a two-year training program. Entry-level environmental conservation officers (or ECO Trainee 1) first complete a 26-week residential basic training academy, where they learn police skills as well as the technical aspects of environmental law enforcement. They then perform enforcement work while under close supervision by a field training officer. Once they enter the second year of training, ECO Trainees advance to the title of ECO Trainee 2, and at the completion of the second year of training, they receive the full title of environmental conservation officer.

EXPLORING

Visit the Web sites of your state's department of conservation or department of natural resources to learn more about conservation work and issues in your region. Another great way to learn about conservation officer careers is by reading books such as *The Thin Green Line: A Thumbnail Sketch of the Career of a Wildlife Conservation Officer in Rural Pennsylvania*, by Rick Larnerd; and *Saving the Earth as a Career: Advice on Becoming a Conservation Professional*, by Malcolm L. Hunter Jr., et al. And you can watch conservation officers in action on New York State's "DEC TV" Web site (http://www.dec.ny.gov/dectv/dectv74.html).

EMPLOYERS

The U.S. Department of Labor reports that approximately 20,000 forest and conservation workers were employed in the United States in 2006. About 34 percent worked for the government, predominantly at the state and local levels. Many worked for the Department of Conservation within their state. The U.S. Fish and Wildlife Service reports that in 2009 it employed 7,500 men and women with a wide range of educational backgrounds and skills.

STARTING OUT

Look for volunteer, internship, and part-time job opportunities with conservation groups. Your state's Department of Natural Resources or Department of Conservation lists volunteer programs and job openings on its Web site. If you don't know the URL, use a search engine and key in the name of your state followed by "department of conservation" or "department of natural resources," and the Web address should appear among the top findings. Helping to clear a trail or pitching in on an educational or promotion program will give you a better idea of what's involved in conservation work. Getting your foot in the door early also gives you the chance to speak with people who are already working in the field, to find out how they got started and what their day-to-day tasks are like.

You can also try to get a summer job with the U.S. Fish and Wildlife Service (FWS). These are popular jobs that fill quickly, so make sure you apply early. Applications are accepted usually between January and April for jobs available that summer. Visit the FWS Web site to learn more about job openings (http://www.fws.gov/jobs/index.htm).

ADVANCEMENT

Conservation officers can advance to supervisor positions within their area, and later to director positions that cover multiple areas. They may branch out by entering the higher education field, teaching college and university students about conservation practices and laws. They may also write books and articles about their experiences and philosophies on environmental and wildlife conservation.

EARNINGS

Conservation officers' salaries vary based on experience. For example, the New York State Department of Environmental Conservation lists 2009 salaries for environmental conservation officers as follows:

- ECO Trainee 1 (entry-level): starting salary is $42,107
- Upon completion of 30 weeks of training, ECO Trainee 1 salary increases to $44,124
- After completing an additional 22 weeks of training and advancing to ECO Trainee 2 level, salary increases to $46,181
- At the completion of a two-year traineeship, salary increases to $48,359

Conservation officers that work for the U.S. Fish and Wildlife Service are paid according to federal pay scales, which are referred to as "general schedule" or GS. GS salaries can range from $29,656 for entry-level positions to $91,000 or more for advanced positions.

WORK ENVIRONMENT

Conservation officers work indoors in offices, writing reports, conducting research on the Internet, and fielding email and phone calls. They also speak at schools and community meetings and events. Much of their workday may be spent outdoors, inspecting the area they're assigned to, inventorying species and taking notes on people's activities, as well as leading educational workshops. They may travel to conduct investigations, serve warrants, and arrest people. Every day is different and job tasks vary regularly. They work outdoors in any kind of weather; so physical strength and stamina are required to handle the job.

OUTLOOK

The U.S. Department of Labor does not forecast specifically for conservation officer careers, but expects average employment growth through 2016 for law enforcement workers such as police and detectives. Employment in the conservation enforcement field depends on state and federal budgets, which vary every year. Job opportunities will also vary by region. Some areas of the country are extremely popular for conservation work, and competition for jobs is usually keen, with applicants far outnumbering the positions that are available. Candidates with wildlife conservation experience and/or a military background will have better odds of securing work.

FOR MORE INFORMATION

The New York State Department of Environmental Conservation was created in 1970 to help protect the state's natural resources and environment. Find online newsletters, events calendars, and more by visiting

New York State Department of Environmental Conservation
625 Broadway
Albany, NY 12233-0001
http://www.dec.ny.gov

Founded in 1980, this organization consists of 8,000 members who are wildlife and fisheries enforcement officials throughout North America. Learn more about membership, conferences, and events by visiting NAWEOA's Web site.

North American Wildlife Enforcement Officers Association (NAWEOA)
http://www.naweoa.org

Find out more about wildlife conservation and job and volunteer opportunities by visiting the Web sites of the following federal organizations:

U.S. Fish and Wildlife Service
Department of the Interior
1849 C Street, NW
Washington, DC 20240-0001
Tel: 800-344-9453
http://www.fws.gov

U.S. National Park Service
Department of the Interior
1849 C Street, NW

Washington, DC 20240-0001
Tel: 202-208-6843
http://www.nps.gov

Learn more about membership, events, and volunteer opportunities by visiting

Wildlife Conservation Society
2300 Southern Boulevard
Bronx, NY 10460-1068
Tel: 718-220-5100
http://www.wcs.org

Environmental Engineers

 QUICK FACTS

School Subjects
Mathematics
Physics

Personal Skills
Leadership/management
Technical/scientific

Work Environment
Indoors and outdoors
Primarily multiple locations

Minimum Education Level
Bachelor's degree

Salary Range
$45,310 to $74,020 to
$115,430+

Certification or Licensing
Required

Outlook
Much faster than the average

OVERVIEW

Environmental engineers design, build, and maintain systems to control waste streams produced by municipalities or private industry. Such waste streams may be wastewater, solid waste, hazardous waste, or contaminated emissions to the atmosphere (air pollution). Environmental engineers are employed by the Environmental Protection Agency (EPA), private industry, or engineering consulting firms.

HISTORY

Although people have been doing work that falls into the category of environmental engineering for decades, it is only within about the last 30 years that a separate professional category has been recognized for environmental engineers.

Post-Civil War industrialization and urbanization created life-threatening water and air quality problems. These problems continued during and after World War II, dramatically increasing all forms of environmental pollution. After the war, pollution control technologies were developed to deal with the damage.

From the 1930s until about the 1960s, sanitary engineering was the title used for what is now commonly known as environmental engineering, and its focus in the early days was on wastewater and sewers. Sanitary engineering is a form of civil engineering. "Civil engineering is engineering for municipalities," explains Michael Waxman, Ph.D., who is a professor and program director at the University of Wisconsin—Madison College of Engineering. "It includes things like building roads, highways, [and] buildings. But a big part of civil engineering is dealing with the waste streams that come from cities or municipalities. Wastewater from a city's sewage treatment plants is a prime example," Waxman says. This water must be treated in order to be pure enough to be used again. "Scientists work out what must be done to break down the harmful substances in the water, such as by adding bacteria; engineers design, build, and maintain the systems needed to carry this out. Technicians monitor the systems, take samples, run tests, and otherwise ensure that the system is working as it should.

"This structure—scientists deciding what should be done at the molecular or biological level, engineers designing the systems needed to carry out the project, and technicians taking care of the day-to-day monitoring of the systems—is applied to other waste streams as well," Waxman adds.

Environmental engineering is an offshoot of civil engineering/sanitary engineering and focuses on the development of the physical systems needed to control waste streams. Civil engineers who already were doing this type of work began to refer to themselves as environmental engineers around 1970 with the great boom in new environmental regulations, according to Waxman. "It's what they wanted to be called," he says. "They wanted the recognition for what they were doing."

THE JOB

Consider the following hypothetical situation: There is a small pond in Crawford County, Illinois, which provides the habitat and primary food source for several different species of fish, frogs, turtles, insects, and birds, as well as small mammals. About a half-mile away is the Jack J. Ryan and Sons Manufacturing Company. For years, this plant has safely treated its wastewater—produced during the manufacturing process—and discharged it into the pond. Then one day, without warning, hundreds of dead fish wash up on the banks of the pond. What's going on? What should be done? It is the job of environmental engineers to investigate and design a system to make the water safe for the flora and fauna that depend on it for survival.

Environmental engineers who work for the federal or state EPA act as police officers or detectives. They investigate problems stemming from systems that aren't functioning properly. They have knowledge about wastewater treatment systems and have the authority to enforce environmental regulations.

The Crawford County pond is in the jurisdiction of the Champaign regional office of the Illinois Environmental Protection Agency (IEPA). There are three divisions: air, land, and water. An environmental engineer in the water division would be alerted to the fish kill at the pond and head out to the site to investigate. The engineer takes photographs and samples of the water and makes notes to document the problem. He or she considers the possibilities: Is it a discharge problem from Jack J. Ryan and Sons? If so, was there an upset in the process? A spill? A flood? Could a storage tank be leaking? Or is the problem further upstream? The pond is connected to other waterways, so could some other discharger be responsible for killing the fish?

The engineer visits Jack J. Ryan and Sons to talk to the production manager and ask if the plant has been doing anything differently lately. The investigation might include a tour of the plant or an examination of its plans. It might also include questioning other manufacturers further upstream, to see if they are doing something new that has caused the fish deaths.

Once the problem has been identified, the environmental engineer and the plant officials can work together on the solution. For example, the production manager at Jack J. Ryan and Sons reports that they've changed something in the manufacturing process to produce a new kind of die-cast part. They didn't know they were doing something wrong. The EPA engineer informs the company they'll be fined $10,000, and a follow-up investigation will be conducted to make sure it has complied with regulations.

Jack J. Ryan and Sons may have its own environmental engineer on staff. This engineer's job is to help keep the company in compliance with federal and state regulations while balancing the economic concerns of the company. At one time, industries' environmental affairs positions were often filled by employees who also had other positions. Since the late 1980s, however, these positions are held by environmental experts, including scientists, engineers, lawyers, and communications professionals.

An environmental engineer assembles a sensor used to measure gaseous emissions. *Maximilian Stock Ltd./Photo Researchers, Inc.*

In the Crawford County pond scenario, a Ryan and Sons environmental expert might get a call from an engineer at the IEPA: "There seems to be a fish kill at the pond near your plant. We've determined it's probably from a discharge from your plant." The Jack J. Ryan and Sons expert looks at the plant's plans, talks to the production manager, and figures out a plan of action to bring the company into compliance.

Some companies rely on environmental engineering consulting firms instead of keeping an engineer on staff. Consulting firms usually provide teams that visit the plant, assess the problem, and design a system to get the plant back into compliance. Consulting firms not only know the technical aspects of waste control, but also have expertise in dealing with the government—filling out the required government forms, for example.

Broadly speaking, environmental engineers may focus on one of three areas: air, land, or water. Those who are concerned with air work on air pollution control, air quality management, and other specialties involved in systems to treat emissions. The private sector tends to have the majority of these jobs, according to the Environmental Careers Organization. Environmental engineers focused on land include landfill professionals, for whom environmental engineering and public health are key areas. Engineers focused on water work on activities similar to those described in the forementioned Jack J. Ryan and Sons scenario.

A big responsibility for environmental engineers is hazardous waste management. Expertise in designing systems and processes to reduce, recycle, and treat hazardous waste streams is very much in demand. This area tends to be the most technical of all the environmental fields and so demands more professionals with graduate and technical degrees.

Environmental engineers spend a lot of time on paperwork, including writing reports and memos and filling out forms. They also might climb a smokestack, wade in a creek, or go toe-to-toe with a district attorney in a battle over a compliance matter. If they work on company staffs, they may face frustration over not knowing what is going on in their own plants. If they work for the government, they might struggle with bureaucracy. If they work for a consultant, they may have to juggle the needs of the client (including the need to keep costs down) with the demands of the government.

REQUIREMENTS
High School
A bachelor's degree is mandatory to work in environmental engineering. At the high school level, the most important course work is in science and mathematics. It's also good to develop written communication skills. Competition to get into the top engineering schools is tough, so it's important to do well on ACT or SAT tests.

Postsecondary Training
About 20 schools offer an undergraduate degree in environmental engineering. Another possibility is to earn a civil engineering, mechanical engineering, industrial engineering, or other traditional engineering degree with an environmental focus. You could also obtain a traditional engineering degree and learn the environmental knowledge on the job, or obtain a master's degree in environmental engineering.

Certification or Licensing

If your work as an engineer affects public health, safety, or property, you must register with the state. To obtain registration, you must have a degree from an accredited engineering program. Right before you get your degree (or soon after), you must pass an engineer in training (EIT) exam covering fundamentals of science and engineering. A few years after you've started your career, you also must pass an exam covering engineering practice. Additional certification is voluntary and may be obtained through such organizations as the American Academy of Environmental Engineers.

Other Requirements

Environmental engineers must like solving problems and have a good background in science and math. They must be able to, in the words of one engineer, "Just get in there and figure out what needs to be done." Engineers must be able to communicate verbally and in writing with a variety of people from both technical and nontechnical backgrounds.

EXPLORING

A good way to explore becoming an environmental engineer is to talk to someone in the field. Contact your local EPA office, use a Web search engine to look for environmental consulting firms in your area, or ask a local industrial company if you can visit. The latter is not as far-fetched as you might think: Big industry has learned the value of positive community relations, and their outreach efforts may include having an open house for their neighbors in which one can walk through their plants, ask questions, and get a feel for what goes on there.

You cannot be a practicing environmental engineer without having a bachelor's degree. However, you can put yourself in situations in which you're around environmental engineers to see what they do and how they work. To do so, you may volunteer for the local chapter of a nonprofit environmental organization, do an internship through ECO or another organization, or work first as an environmental technician, a job that requires less education (such as a two-year associate's degree or even a high school diploma).

Another good way to get exposure to environmental engineering is to familiarize yourself with professional journals. Two journals that may be available in your library or that you can read online include *Chemical & Engineering News* (http://pubs. acs.org/cen), which regularly features articles on waste management systems, and *Pollution Engineering* (http://www.pollution engineering.com), which features articles of interest to environmental engineers.

EMPLOYERS

Approximately 54,000 environmental engineers are employed in the United States. Environmental engineers most often work for the EPA, in private industry, or at engineering consulting firms. In 2006 approximately 29 percent of all environmental engineers employed in the United States worked in architectural, engineering, and related services, according to the U.S. Department of Labor.

STARTING OUT

The traditional method of entering this field is by obtaining a bachelor's degree and applying directly to companies or to the EPA. School career services offices can assist you in these efforts. You can also get a better idea of the types of environmental engineers companies are hiring by reading the job descriptions on such employment Web sites such as ECO (http://www.eco.org), Environmental Engineer (http://www.environmentalengineer.com), Environmental Career Opportunities (http://www.ecojobs.com), and Simply Hired (http://www.simplyhired.com), to name only a few.

ADVANCEMENT

After environmental engineers have gained work experience, there are several routes for advancement. Those working for the EPA can become a department supervisor or switch to private industry or consulting. In-house environmental staff members may rise to supervisory positions. Engineers with consulting firms may become project managers or specialists in certain areas.

Environmental careers are evolving at a breakneck speed. New specialties are emerging all the time. Advancement may take the form of getting involved at the beginning stages of a new subspecialty that suits an engineer's particular interests, experience, and expertise.

WORDS TO KNOW

biodegradation The use of bacteria or other living organisms to decompose contaminants.

Comprehensive Environmental Response, Compensation, and Liability Act (CERCLA) A 1980 law (known as "Superfund") that mandated cleanup of private and government-owned hazardous waste sites.

corrosive waste A waste that corrodes steel at a rate greater than 6.35 millimeters (0.25 inches) per year, or that is outside the pH range of 2 to 12.5. Corrosive waste is one of the four hazardous waste properties of the EPA.

EPA U.S. Environmental Protection Agency—the federal agency responsible for overseeing the implementation of environmental laws, including those designed to monitor and control air, water, and soil pollution. State EPAs help enforce these laws.

HAPs Hazardous air pollutants.

hazardous waste Any discarded substance, usually chemicals, that can cause harm to humans.

landfill A legal and controlled area in which to place wastes into the ground.

National Priorities List U.S. EPA list of the worst hazardous waste sites in the country needing cleanup.

remediation The process by which environmental problems are remedied or redressed.

septic Anaerobic (without air) decomposition typically accompanied by an unpleasant odor.

EARNINGS

The U.S. Department of Labor reports that median annual earnings of environmental engineers were $74,020 in 2008. Salaries ranged from less than $45,310 for the lowest paid 10 percent to more than $115,430 for the highest paid 10 percent. According to a 2007 salary survey by the National Association of Colleges and Employers, bachelor's degree candidates in environmental health received starting offers averaging $47,960 a year.

Fringe benefits vary widely depending on the employer. State EPA jobs may include, for example, two weeks of vacation, health insurance, tuition reimbursement, use of company vehicles for work, and similar perks. In-house or consulting positions may add additional benefits to lure top candidates.

WORK ENVIRONMENT

Environmental engineers split their time between working in an office and working out in the field. They may also spend time in courtrooms. Since ongoing education is crucial in most of these positions, engineers must attend training sessions and workshops and study new regulations, techniques, and problems. Environmental engineers usually work as part of a team that may include any of a number of different specialists. They must also give presentations of technical information to those with both technical and nontechnical backgrounds.

OUTLOOK

The *Occupational Outlook Handbook* projects that employment for environmental engineers will grow much faster than the average for all occupations through 2016. According to the American Academy of Environmental Engineers, "Since the turn of the century, there have always been more jobs than environmental engineers to fill them." Engineers will be needed to clean up existing hazards and help companies comply with government regulations. The shift toward prevention of problems and protecting public health should continue to create job opportunities.

Jobs are available with all three major employers—the EPA, private industry, and consulting firms. The EPA has long been a major employer of environmental engineers.

FOR MORE INFORMATION

For information on certification, careers, and salaries or a copy of Environmental Engineering Selection Guide *(giving names of accredited environmental engineering programs and of professors who have board certification as environmental engineers), contact*

American Academy of Environmental Engineers
130 Holiday Court, Suite 100
Annapolis, MD 21401-7003

Tel: 410-266-3311
http://www.aaee.net

For information on internships and career guidance, visit ECO's Web site at
Environmental Careers Organization
http://www.eco.org

Learn more about job responsibilities and the types of companies that hire environmental engineers by visiting the following Web site:
Get Environmental Engineering Jobs
http://www.getenvironmentalengineeringjobs.com

For career guidance information, contact
Junior Engineering Technical Society
1420 King Street, Suite 405
Alexandria, VA 22314-2794
Tel: 703-548-5387
Email: info@jets.org
http://www.jets.org

The following is a cross-disciplinary environmental association:
National Association of Environmental Professionals
PO Box 460
Collingswood, NJ 08108-0460
Tel: 856-283-7816
http://www.naep.org

For information about the private waste services industry, contact
National Solid Wastes Management Association
4301 Connecticut Avenue, NW, Suite 300
Washington, DC 20008-2304
Tel: 202-244-4700
http://www.nswma.org

Contact SCA for information about internships for high school students.
Student Conservation Association (SCA)
689 River Road
PO Box 550
Charlestown, NH 03603-0550
Tel: 603-543-1700
http://www.sca-inc.org

Environmental Health Officers

OVERVIEW

Environmental health officers are usually hired by public health departments to inspect public and private sites to make sure business operations and processes, as well as the environments themselves, comply with environmental health laws. They regularly inspect such sites as restaurants, schools, manufacturing plants and factories, apartment buildings, and recreational facilities. They visit sites, conduct tests, take samples, and write reports regarding their findings. They may serve citations and appear in court to testify on certain cases.

HISTORY

For centuries, cities large and small faced various environmental health problems, including air pollution from wood smoke, dust, and animal manure; and water and land pollution from sewage and other waste. Smog and other serious environmental issues existed long before the mid-1800s, but when the industrial revolution began in England and later in America, pollution was taken to new, astronomical levels. Manufacturing plants emitted carbon particles into the air in such dense amounts that thick, black clouds of smoke blanketed cities and surrounding areas. (Smoke + fog = smog. This was the origin of the name.) Many people suffered and died from respiratory diseases during this time. Waterways were also extremely polluted. Factories dumped toxic waste into rivers; and cities dumped sewage and domestic waste into waters. Epidemics from water-borne diseases such as cholera and typhoid fever killed thousands of people, particularly poor people who often lived in the more polluted areas and who had few resources to sustain themselves. British physician John Snow was an early founder of medical hygiene, a division of the environmental health field; in 1854 he made the connection that cholera deaths in the Soho area of London were directly linked to pollution in the Thames River.

At the turn of the 20th century, concern grew about the environments in which people lived and worked, the quality and condition of food and drinking water, sanitation, and the industries that were causing pollution. The United States passed the Pure Food and Drugs Act in 1906 to protect people from hazardous foods and medicines, and established the National Institute (now Institutes) of Health in 1930 to conduct health research and help prevent disease and illness.

After World War II, focus returned to environmental health. The Environmental Protection Agency was established in 1970 to control pollution, set standards, and protect human health and the environment. Numerous environmental and health laws have been passed since the 1970s to improve air and water quality, control the disposal of hazardous waste, reduce noise, and improve quality of life. The World Health Organization states in its 2006 report, "Preventing Disease through Healthy Environments," that about 25 percent of global disease can be attributed to environmental exposures, and environmental factors are responsible for 23 percent of all deaths. Research and development continues regarding the effects of emissions from fossil fuels and exposure to other chemicals on the environment and human health. And environmental health professionals are needed to enforce laws and regulations, as well as help introduce new procedures to improve the quality of life.

THE JOB

Environmental health officers help to protect the health of populations, preventing the spread of illness and disease by inspecting various sites and assessing potential health risks. They may specialize in food safety, industrial hygiene, injury prevention and education, epidemiological surveillance, radiological health, disease prevention, and emergency preparedness. They also investigate public health outbreaks to help determine causes. If they work for smaller organizations, they may work independently; in larger organizations, they typically work with a team of environmental health officers.

Much of their work involves traveling to sites and inspecting the ways in which businesses operate and the state of the environment in which they operate. The officers may schedule these visits in advance, giving the business owner forewarning, or they may show up spontaneously, not allowing the business owner any time to potentially "clean up" whatever may be in violation of environmental health codes. If they specialize in food safety, for example, they inspect restaurants to see how food is stored and cooked, how the staff handles the food, and how the flatware and utensils and glasses are cleaned. They also observe the overall cleanliness of the restaurant, looking for signs of rodents and bugs. They may collect food samples for testing in laboratories. For food manufacturing companies, environmental health officers inspect the quality and freshness of the products that are packaged, as well as the manufacturing and packaging processes and the cleanliness of the plant.

Environmental health officers make sure recreational facilities are maintained and operated according to health laws and regulations. For instance, they may inspect community swimming pools, review cleaning schedules, and test the water in the pools for chlorine levels. They also inspect factories and water disposal facilities to determine the impact these business operations have on air and water quality, and the levels of noise and pollution. If they suspect violations, they may take water and soil samples. And if laboratory analyses show pollution in excess of environmental standards, health officers may issue an order to the business owner to reduce pollution levels. They meet with business owners or those responsible for the business to discuss the findings from the inspection and review where improvements, if any, need to be made, and issue a citation if necessary. They visit the site again to ensure corrections have been made to bring the environment up to standard. If corrections are not made and violations are repeated, environmental health officers can file a court complaint, in which the owner will have to appear before a judge, and health officers may also need to testify about their findings.

Taking detailed notes during inspections, and summarizing these notes into written reports (often dubbed "report cards"), is a major part of the job of being an environmental health officer.

These reports are often made public—and often shared through the media—so the ability to state facts and findings clearly and succinctly is essential. Solid communication skills are also important in the job because officers may be called upon to conduct educational programs regarding environmental health and safety issues. They also keep up with research and development in the environmental health field, and make recommendations for new processes and procedures to improve environmental health.

Responding to environmental crises is another area in which environmental health officers may work. Preparing and training for emergencies has become a part of many environmental health officers' jobs. They may train people in how to handle and respond to a disaster. Depending on their expertise and employer, they may be assigned to work in third-world countries to help in the aftermath of environmental crises and provide safety to military troops.

REQUIREMENTS

High School
While in high school, take classes in biology, chemistry, physics, environmental studies, history, math, English, and computers. Foreign language classes are also beneficial.

Postsecondary Training
A bachelor's degree is usually required to work as an environmental health officer. Many employers prefer to hire officers who have an advanced degree. Course work includes the sciences, such as biology, microbiology, environmental science, and food science; public or environmental health; and health protection or public health inspection. Students also study environmental health laws, regulations, policies, and procedures.

Certification or Licensing
Environmental health officers are required to be certified at the state or national level. Certification can be obtained through the National Environmental Health Association. The standard designation in the profession is registered environmental health specialist, or registered sanitarian. A bachelor's degree in environmental or public health, or a degree in another field coupled with two years of work experience, is required to take the certification exam.

Other Requirements
The ability to handle working long hours while dealing with a variety of personalities (some not always friendly) is essential to

succeeding in this job. Physical fitness helps for the days spent visiting and inspecting sites. Self-motivation is required as much of the work is done independently. Diplomacy is also essential, especially if working in disaster areas and with people from foreign countries.

EXPLORING

Professional associations offer plenty of resources and ways to learn more about the environmental health field. Visit their Web sites and look for the calendar section to see if there are upcoming events in your region that spark your interest, such as a conference or workshop. You can also get a better idea about environmental health issues and the work involved in remedying environmental problems by reading publications such as the *National Environmental Health Association's Journal of Environmental Health*, and books such as *Environmental Health: From Global to Local*, by Howard Frumkin.

EMPLOYERS

Environmental health officers work for federal and state departments of health. The Commissioned Corps of the United States Public Health Service (PHS) also employs many environmental health officers, who are supported by the Chief Environmental Health Officer and the Office of the Surgeon General. According to the U.S. Bureau of Labor Statistics, about 56,000 occupational health and safety specialists were employed in the United States in 2006, with about two out of every five specialists working for government agencies. Environmental health officers also work for private general medical and surgical hospitals; private consulting and manufacturing firms; colleges, universities, and professional schools; scientific and technical consulting services; research and development companies; and insurance groups.

STARTING OUT

An internship or a part-time job is an excellent way to get started in an environmental health career. Check the Web site of your state's department of public health for internships and job listings. You can also find job postings on the American Public Health Association's Web site (http://apha.org/career) and on the National Environmental Health Association's Web site (http://www.neha.org/job_center.html).

ADVANCEMENT

Environmental health officers can advance to positions of greater authority, such as supervisor, department head, regional director, and senior specialist. With advanced degrees and years of work experience, they can become professors or research and write about environmental health.

EARNINGS

Salaries for environmental health officers vary depending upon their level of experience and the type of employer. The U.S. Department of Labor (DoL) reports that salaries in 2008 for occupational health and safety specialists ranged from $35,870 to $93,620, with a median income of $62,250. Specialists working for the federal government in 2008 had median annual incomes of $73,470, while those who worked for the state government earned $57,440 per year. Occupational health and safety specialists who worked for management, scientific, and technical consulting services, or general medical and surgical hospitals earned about $63,975 per year. In 2008 the top-paying metropolitan areas for this job were Knoxville, Tennessee; Columbus, Ohio; Framingham, Massachusetts; San Francisco, California; and Olympia, Washington. Salary.com shows annual salaries for health and safety managers in 2009 as ranging from $83,833 to $147,344 or more, with $114,230 as the median annual income.

WORK ENVIRONMENT

Environmental health officers work 40 or more hours per week in offices and at the sites they are inspecting. For example, they may spend a good part of their day in restaurant kitchens, factories, or even mines. Their workweeks are irregular, and the job can be stressful because they are frequently exposed to the same environmental dangers and stressors that they investigate. They may also have to deal with irate business owners or managers who are unhappy about having their businesses inspected and angry if they receive a poor "report card."

OUTLOOK

Employment of environmental health officers is expected to grow about as fast as the average for all occupations through 2016.

New, and sometimes amended, environmental health laws and regulations are enacted regularly due to increased awareness of health hazards in the workplace, schools, hospitals, and other public environments. With tighter restrictions, more environmental health officers may be needed to help ensure compliance by businesses and business owners. In addition, emergency preparedness has taken on greater importance throughout the past decade and is another area in which environmental health officers will be needed in years to come. Jobs will also arise from officers retiring from the field or leaving their jobs to pursue other employment opportunities.

FOR MORE INFORMATION

Learn more about environmental health careers by visiting
American Public Health Association
800 I Street, NW
Washington, DC 20001-3710
Tel: 202-777-2742
http://apha.org

The following is a cross-disciplinary environmental association:
National Association of Environmental Professionals
PO Box 460
Collingswood, NJ 08108-0460
Tel: 856-283-7816
http://www.naep.org

Find information about membership, job listings, upcoming events, and industry news by visiting NEHA's Web site.
National Environmental Health Association (NEHA)
720 South Colorado Boulevard, Suite 1000-N
Denver, CO 80246-1926
Tel: 866-956-2258
Email: staff@neha.org
http://www.neha.org

Find student opportunities in environmental health and read environmental health officers' bios on the HHS's Web site.
U.S. Department of Health and Human Services (HHS)
1101 Wootton Parkway, Plaza Level
Rockville, MD 20852-1059

Tel: 877-463–6327
http://www.usphs.gov

Learn more about research projects and education programs by visiting NIH's Web site.

U.S. Department of Health and Human Services
National Institutes of Health (NIH)
9000 Rockville Pike
Bethesda, MD 20892-0001
Tel: 301-496-4000
Email: NIHinfo@od.nih.gov
http://www.nih.gov

Environmental Lawyers

OVERVIEW

Environmental lawyers deal with environmental law, which has to do with federal and state regulations that concern wildlife, endangered species, habitats, public lands, logging and forestry, natural resources, hazardous and toxic wastes, air and water pollution, and other environment-related statutes. Environmental lawyers work either for the government or private sector and are hired to help bring cases to court to enforce environmental regulations and to alter public and private activities that may be damaging the environment. They research and prepare legal cases, interviewing various people involved in the case, as well as experts in the field, such as scientists and engineers, to help substantiate the case. They also present cases in court.

HISTORY

The first federal environmental law—the Rivers and Harbors Act—was enacted by Congress in 1899 and signed into law by President William McKinley. The act was created to protect waters from pollution and to also protect the navigability of waters. The discharge of refuse of any kind into U.S. navigable waters or tributaries without a permit is deemed a misdemeanor under this law. The act also deems it a misdemeanor if excavation, filling, or altering has been done, without a permit, to the course, condition, or capacity of any channel, harbor, port, or other water areas as described in the act. Many other older environmental acts have since been incorporated under the Clean Water Act, but the Rivers and Harbors Act remains independent and vital, administered today by the U.S. Army Corps of Engineers. It continues to safeguard waters, and has provided the basis for numerous lawsuits filed by state agencies and the Environmental Protection Agency against corporations that have discharged pollutants and hazardous wastes into rivers and harbors.

President Theodore Roosevelt was passionate about the environment and conserving wild lands, and was instrumental in getting many conservation laws passed during his two terms in office (1901–1909). Under Roosevelt's administration, the protection of national forest acreage multiplied five times over, from 40 million acres to 200 million acres. And the National Parks and Monument Act for the Preservation of American Antiquities (known as the Antiquities Act) was passed in 1906, a landmark environmental law intended to preserve archaeological sites on public lands and requiring federal agencies to manage and preserve these natural resources. The Antiquities Act authorizes the president to publicly proclaim, at his discretion, historic landmarks, historic and prehistoric structures, and other objects of scientific or historic interest, which are on federally controlled lands, as national monuments and to preserve the lands on which they are located.

An early lawsuit in U.S. environmental law history was the case of *Scenic Hudson Preservation v. Federal Power Commission (FPC)* in 1965. Con Edison had plans to build a power plant on scenic and historic Storm King Mountain, near the Hudson River in New York. A group of residents opposed the plans and organized to protect the land; the case gathered strength when conservation groups joined the fight. The attorney representing the residents argued not on technical aspects (such as regarding Con Edison's ability to carry out its plans), but rather on aesthetic and quality-of-life aspects, charging that the FPC had not adequately addressed the interests of the public, meaning Storm King Mountain's beauty and historical importance. The court ruled in favor of Scenic Hudson Preservation, and the case is considered a landmark in environmental law because it was the first time a conservation group was allowed to sue to protect public interest.

In the 1970s interest in the environment continued to grow, triggering the passing of many environmental laws, such as the

Endangered Species Act, the Toxic Substances Control Act, and the Environmental Pesticide Control Act, as well as amendments to the Clean Air Act and the Clean Water Act. The U.S. government committed to protect the health of the environment and its inhabitants when, in 1970, it enacted the National Environmental Policy Act and established the Environmental Protection Agency. Environmental law has expanded in the decades since to match the growth of environmental policy and legislation.

THE JOB

The environmental law field is large, consisting of several main areas of concentration (air, land, water), categories within these concentrations (such as water pollution), and even further subcategories (such as hazardous waste). Environmental lawyers work for private or government sectors. Depending on the case, their tasks involve either defending clients or prosecuting other parties. Private-sector lawyers typically defend and represent businesses that are facing government action over environmental concerns. Government lawyers, on the other hand, work to enforce environmental laws and regulations. Their work entails prosecuting the parties that are responsible for pollution or other environmental transgressions in violation of federal law.

As mentioned in the previous section, numerous environmental laws and regulations exist to protect land, air, water, wildlife, and human beings. Environmental lawyers must know environmental legislation well to successfully build and defend cases. In addition to the Clean Air Act and Clean Water Act, other policies that they frequently refer to in their work include the Emergency Planning and Community Right to Know Act; Hazardous Materials Transportation Authorization Act; Resource Conservation and Recovery Act; Safe Drinking Water Act; and the Comprehensive Environmental Response, Compensation, and Liability Act (CERCLA)— more commonly known as Superfund.

Environmental lawyers who begin their careers in government agencies usually receive lower salaries, but they gain more experience because they are usually directly involved in cases. In the private sector, senior lawyers typically handle the cases, relegating beginning lawyers to the back seat. Government lawyers may work within city and state attorneys' offices; with air, water, and land bureaus within state environmental protection agencies; and with federal agencies such as the U.S. Environmental Protection Agency. Federal, state, and local agencies collaborate by sharing resources and information to better enforce environmental protection laws. They prosecute many different types of environmental crimes, from air pollution to wildlife endangerment. Government environmental lawyers help in the pursuit of civil and criminal actions to enforce ordinances, statutes, and regulations at the federal, state, and city levels. Cases range from environmental remediation to public nuisance abatements and injunctions regarding matters such as lead-based paint. Government agencies also work closely with public interest or environmental advocacy organizations.

Private sector environmental lawyers help corporate clients with such matters as environmental defense, compliance, and risk. They deal with mergers, acquisitions, and real estate transactions, and provide advice, counsel, and strategy development. Cases they work on may involve such environmental issues as indoor air quality, land use and natural resources, solid and hazardous waste management, or brownfield restoration and site remediation. (A brownfield is an abandoned industrial or commercial site that may be contaminated but has potential for reuse.) Environmental cleanup cases are especially complicated and stressful—private and government attorneys are typically on opposite sides of the fence regarding who is responsible for the cleanup. Environmental laws are also not always clear, which can further complicate matters. Early environmental laws required companies to clean up all contaminants they had introduced to the environment. In the past decade, however, laws have evolved that enable companies to remove contaminants to the point where they are at an "acceptable level," and where they pose no immediate threat to human health and the environment. This does not mean laws have gotten lax over the years, but rather that knowledge has increased regarding "natural attenuation"—a process by which contaminants naturally diffuse over time.

Environmental lawyers may also work for small, specialized environmental law firms. They may also start their own private practice, as solo attorneys or in partnership with other attorneys. Some pursue public interest work, providing services for national groups that frequently rely on legal representation to accomplish their goals, such as the Sierra Club. Some environmental attorneys find jobs as in-house counsels for large corporations, such as waste disposal firms and chemical companies. In-house counsel means that they don't exclusively represent their employers, but, rather, they work closely with other environmental attorneys at private firms who are well-versed in particular concentrations of environmental law, and can lend further expertise based on their knowledge of the local politics, culture, and laws, as well as the local authorities themselves.

REQUIREMENTS
High School
Classes in biology, chemistry, environmental studies, history, economics, English, computers, and foreign language are a solid basis for undergraduate studies in environmental law. Course work that emphasizes research, analytical thinking, and writing is recommended. The ability to argue a case and speak well in public is crucial to success in this job. Speech and debate classes will help hone your skills in this area.

Postsecondary Training
An undergraduate degree from an accredited college or university is required to practice environmental law. Bachelor's degree studies can be in a range of subjects. Environmental lawyers may have educational backgrounds in biology, political science, English, environmental policy, or agriculture. Science and engineering studies are especially useful because environmental law work involves reading and understanding scientific explanations about pollutants and other environmental issues.

Upon receiving their undergraduate degree, students take the LSAT (Law School Admission Test) to gain entrance to a law school accredited by the American Bar Association. They attend law school for three years, taking classes that cover such topics as legal methods, civil procedure, criminal law and criminal procedure, and torts. Environmental law students also receive specialized training through internships with private law firms, government agencies, or nonprofit organizations that specialize in environmental law. Students who graduate from law school receive a juris doctor (JD) degree.

Certification or Licensing
Courts in all U.S. states and jurisdictions require lawyers to be licensed, or admitted to the bar, as dictated by the rules of the jurisdiction's highest court. Bar admission applicants are required to pass a written bar examination. In nearly all states, applicants must also pass a separate written ethics examination. Some states may require lawyers who have passed the bar in a different state to take their state's bar examination if they wish to practice law there. Other states may not require that lawyers take a second bar exam, providing the lawyers meet the jurisdiction's good moral character standards and have already practiced law for a certain amount of time. Requirements will vary by state, and federal courts and

agencies set their own qualifications for those practicing before or in them.

To qualify for the bar examination in most states, an applicant must earn a college degree and graduate from a law school accredited by the American Bar Association (ABA) or the proper state authorities. ABA accreditation is important because it means that the law school (especially its library and faculty) meets certain standards. Those who graduate from schools not approved by the ABA (most of these schools are in California) are usually restricted to taking the bar examination and practicing in the state or other jurisdiction in which the school is located.

A nationwide bar examination does not exist, but 48 states, the District of Columbia, Guam, the Northern Mariana Islands, Puerto Rico, and the Virgin Islands require what is known as the Multistate Bar Examination (MBE) as part of their overall bar examination. (Louisiana and Washington do not require the MBE.) The MBE is a six-hour test that covers a broad range of issues. Sometimes a locally prepared state bar examination is given along with the MBE. Several states use the Multistate Essay Examination (MEE), a three-hour test, as part of the bar examination.

In addition to all of the above, many states also mandate Multistate Performance Testing to test the practical skills of beginning lawyers. Requirements vary by state, but this is a one-time requirement and is usually taken at the same time as the bar exam.

Starting in 2007, law school graduates in 52 jurisdictions were required to pass the Multistate Professional Responsibility Examination (MPRE), which tests their knowledge of the ABA codes on professional responsibility and judicial conduct. Some states allow for the MPRE to be taken during law school, usually after completion of a legal ethics course.

Other Requirements

Commitment to environmental issues is essential in practicing environmental law. The ability to deal with massive amounts of paperwork and reading and writing, as well as different types of people from various backgrounds, is critical. Creative, analytical thinking is required, and skill in translating complex information into content that is constructive and persuasive is important in preparing and presenting cases. Strong research skills are intrinsic to the work. Environmental lawyers also spend a great deal of time reading books, magazines, reports, and journals to keep up with developments in the field, news about legal cases, and environmental issues.

EXPLORING

A good first step is to familiarize yourself with the types of projects and issues in which environmental lawyers are involved. Visit MegaLaw for a comprehensive list of environmental law organizations (http://www.megalaw.com/top/envt/envtorg.php), and commit time to checking out the organizations on the list. Keep notes on the topics, programs, and cases that interest you most. You can conduct your own separate search for firms by using an Internet search engine and keying in variations on the words "environmental law firms" and your home state and town.

You will also find plenty of books about environmental legislation in bookstores and through online stores. Try *Environmental Law,* by Nancy Kubasek and Gary Silverman, or *Environmental Law, Policy, and Economics: Reclaiming the Environmental Agenda,* by Nicholas Ashford and Charles Caldart.

EMPLOYERS

According to the U.S. Department of Labor (DoL), about 761,000 lawyers were employed in the United States in 2006, with about 27 percent self-employed in solo practices or practicing as partners in law firms. Many lawyers are employed in full-time, salaried positions in government, law firms or other corporations, or in nonprofit organizations, such as the Natural Resources Defense Council or the Environmental Defense Council. Most government-employed lawyers worked at the local level. Those employed by the federal government work in many different agencies. Lawyers outside of government work as house counsel for public utilities, banks, insurance companies, real estate agencies, manufacturing firms, and other business firms and nonprofit organizations. Some lawyers practice law part time while holding down a job in a different occupation. Lawyers who work for law schools are not included in the statistics as they are part of DoL's separate postsecondary teacher statistics. Some lawyers teach a particular subject at law schools; others work as administrators.

STARTING OUT

Environmental law students secure internships while they are in law school so they can gain firsthand experience in the field. You can get an earlier start by finding a summer or part-time job at an environmental law firm or in the legal department of a nonprofit organization. You can also learn more about environmental defense and law by visiting the Web sites of such groups as the Environmental Defense Fund (http://www.edf.org), which explains more about their work in the Getting the Law Right section, and the Natural Resources Defense Council (http://www.nrdc.org).

ADVANCEMENT

Beginning lawyers start as associates in salaried positions, usually working with more experienced lawyers or judges. With years of experience, they may become partners (partial owners) in their law firm. Government lawyers usually start as interns, moving up to supervisory positions after a few years of practice. With 15 to 20 years of experience, they may become division director or chief legal counsel. Environmental lawyers may also leave salaried positions to start their own law practice. Advancement further down the road can be in the form of nominated or elected judgeships. Lawyers may also pursue academic careers by taking full-time faculty or administrator positions in law schools. Lawyers who work in legal departments of large corporations may gain more experience by taking more senior management positions within their department or working in other departments to gain more exposure to other aspects of the business.

EARNINGS

In 2008 lawyers earned median annual incomes of $110,590, with the lowest salaries starting at $54,460 and the highest incomes at $166,400 or more, based on U.S. Bureau of Labor Statistics findings. Salaries vary based on employer and region. Those who worked for state governments earned $80,890 in 2008. Lawyers employed by local governments averaged about $89,320 annually, and federally employed lawyers brought home $151,820 per year. According to PayScale.com, in 2009 beginning lawyers earned annual salaries ranging from $45,172 to $69,870. Those with five to nine years of experience averaged from $69,065 to $114,515 annually, and lawyers with 10 to 19 years of experience brought home $78,291 to $143,948 per year.

WORK ENVIRONMENT

Environmental lawyers work at least 50 to 60 hours per week, and usually work longer hours that stretch into evenings and weekends when cases are being prepared and tried. Staff lawyers may have more structured hours, while self-employed lawyers may work longer workweeks because of additional administrative responsibilities involved in owning and operating a business.

Lawyers work in offices, law libraries, and courtrooms. They also travel for meetings with clients, and may spend time in clients' business offices, at their homes, or at hospitals or prisons. They visit sites to interview persons of interest and gather research material and evidence. They also travel for meetings and conferences, and appear before courts, legislative bodies, and other authorities.

OUTLOOK

Employment opportunities for lawyers overall are expected to grow about as fast as the average for all occupations through 2016. The Department of Labor (DoL) points out that job growth will be due to increasing demand for legal services in such areas as health care, intellectual property, venture capital, energy, elders, antitrust, and environmental law. Growth will be predominantly in salaried positions in locations where government agencies, big corporations, and law firms are based. The DoL forecasts slower growth in opportunities for self-employed lawyers due to the costs involved in starting a business as well as competition from larger, more established law firms. Stricter environmental laws and regulations will require more lawyers to help defend and enforce environmental issues and policies. Competition continues to be keen in the legal job market in general, however, as there are usually more lawyers than there are available positions. Those who have the flexibility to relocate to different parts of the country for positions will have more opportunities when they search for work.

FOR MORE INFORMATION

Find information about educational requirements to practice law by visiting the ABA's Web site.
American Bar Association (ABA)
321 North Clark Street
Chicago, IL 60654-7598
Tel: 800-285-2221
http://www.abanet.org

Founded in 1967, this organization's first major campaign concerned banning DDT (a strong pesticide) to protect birds. They won that battle and have won many others since. Visit EDF's Web site to learn more about environmental issues and the partnerships EDF is forming to help address them.

Environmental Defense Fund (EDF)
257 Park Avenue South
New York, NY 10010-7304
Tel: 212-505-2100
http://www.edf.org

Learn more about law schools and the Law School Admission Test by visiting

Law School Admission Council
http://www.lsac.org

Find publications, career services, job listings, conferences, and other information at

National Association for Law Placement
1025 Connecticut Avenue, Suite 1110
Washington, DC 20036-5413
Tel: 202-835-1001
Email: info@nalp.org
http://www.nalp.org

Find student projects, volunteer opportunities, and other resources by visiting this organization's Web site.

National Association of Environmental Law Societies
http://www.naels.org

This environmental action group relies on the expertise of more than 350 lawyers, scientists, and other professionals to lobby and litigate on the behalf of environmental issues. Learn more by visiting

Natural Resources Defense Council
40 West 20th Street
New York, NY 10011-4211
Tel: 212-727-2700
http://www.nrdc.org

Environmental Planners

OVERVIEW

Environmental planning is a relatively new field; it emerged in the 1970s in response to the environmental movement. *Environmental planners* are essentially urban planners who focus on sustainable development. They aim to use land in the most efficient way possible, incorporating green building technologies and renewable energy into designs and systems, and preserving ecosystems and environmentally sensitive areas. Planners help manage the growth of cities and ensure that planning designs and systems, such as for construction or transportation projects, are in compliance with federal, state, and local environmental regulations.

HISTORY

Urban planning in the United States dates to the late 17th and early 18th centuries, when cities such as Annapolis, colonial Williamsburg, and Philadelphia were created. In those days cities were laid out in ways to showcase their wealth and power, with focus on the major streets; prominent homes, buildings, and monuments; and large, lush public parks. In 1791 President George Washington assigned the task of planning a new federal capital city to Pierre

Charles L'Enfant, a French-born American architect. For the next year L'Enfant created a plan for the 10-mile square of federal territory that would later be known as Washington, D.C. Heavily influenced by the baroque cities of Europe, he created a gridiron street system that featured diagonal and radial avenues, with the capitol as the main focal point. L'Enfant was fired from the job in 1792 due to frequent conflicts with the commissioners who were appointed to oversee his work. U.S. Surveyor Andrew Ellicott completed the project.

Early *urban planners* placed emphasis on the parts of the city—monuments, buildings, etc.—and not on the city as a whole. Cities that are designed with sole focus on their parts usually suffer when changes occur, and changes in cities occur regularly. The longevity of towns and cities was not taken into account, and thus plans and allowances were not made for such things as population growth and business development. Streets, systems, structures—all were designed to work with life as it was, with the population that existed at the moment designs were created, without much plan for change. Future technologies and systems could not have been foreseen back then, and yet when they developed, cities needed to be renovated or reorganized to best adopt the changes. Automobiles completely altered life and affected the ways in which streets functioned—everything from traffic flow to zoning and land use for storage and parking had to be taken into account and implemented. And cities and towns needed to create and implement plans to effectively bring electricity and telephones to their citizens as well.

Frederick Law Olmsted elevated urban and regional planning to new, professional heights in the 1800s. The designer of many U.S. parks, grounds, and green spaces, including Manhattan's Central Park and Brooklyn's Prospect Park, Olmsted introduced the concept that cities are organic and constantly evolving, and that they consist of interrelated parts that function together to create the whole. He stressed that planners and designers needed to keep all of this in mind when developing their ideas.

The 1916 zoning law that passed in New York also greatly influenced city planning. The first law of its kind to be passed in America, it was created to limit the height of skyscrapers; it also specified the shapes skyscrapers could and could not be, and at which heights the skyscrapers needed to be "set back," to allow for light and air. The "Regional Survey of New York and Environs" in 1929 further introduced considerations for urban and regional planners, such as legal and social factors, as well as internal transit issues.

The environmental movement of the 1960s and 1970s raised awareness about using land more efficiently and responsibly, conserving natural resources and reducing and preventing pollution. Many laws were enacted to address these issues, including the National Environmental Policy Act (NEPA), which had and continues to have a deep impact on planning. Passed in 1969, NEPA requires federal agencies to consider the environmental effects of their proposed actions and come up with reasonable alternatives to those actions. Federal agencies are mandated to prepare an Environmental Impact Statement to verify that their actions are in compliance with NEPA. (The Council of Environmental Quality was also created to ensure that NEPA standards were being met.) After NEPA was enacted, planners started focusing on sustainable development in their work, thinking about the longevity of cities and communities, and factoring in social, ecological, and equity outcomes. The environmental planning field has grown since then. Today, in addition to planning commissions and private-sector consultants working in the field, numerous federal, state, and local government agencies are involved in urban and regional environmental planning projects.

THE JOB

Environmental planners help to ensure that urban and regional development and renovation plans are in compliance with environmental laws and regulations. They analyze plans for potential problems and also look for opportunities. For example, they make sure ecosystems and open spaces will be preserved, that water runoff is managed, and that endangered species are protected. They assess land use, wetlands and habitats, transportation, economic and housing characteristics, flood zones, coastal erosion zones, and air pollution and noise pollution.

Planners create short- and long-term plans for revitalizing and growing urban, suburban, and rural communities and the surrounding regions. In addition to environmental considerations, environmental planners also factor in economic and social health issues of growing communities, and help advise on construction plans for new school buildings, public housing, and other types of infrastructure. Clients also hire planners to help them figure out where to locate roads or new landfills, or for recommendations on zoning regulations.

Environmental planners provide the foundation for responsible development by analyzing and reporting on how land is currently being used for business, residential, and community purposes. Topics that they address in their reports include the location and capacity of highways and streets, schools, libraries, water and sewer lines, airports, and recreational and cultural sites. They also provide data on employment and economic trends, the types of businesses in the area of the prospective development site, and the characteristics of the population and predictions for its rate of growth. They make sure that plans allow for population growth, and that designs of facilities are in keeping with zoning and building codes and environmental regulations. Growing cities and towns also need effective public transportation systems, and planners help develop these systems and present their plans to planning boards and the general public.

Environmental planners may start out as *environmental coordinators* and *associate environmental planners.* A coordinator's responsibilities may include helping to develop plans and policies for natural resources for the coordination of National Environmental Policy Act documents, and participating in, coordinating, or managing natural resources programs and projects. A consulting company in Sacramento, California, was recently seeking to fill an associate environmental planner position for an environmental program. Candidates for the job needed to have prior experience in analyzing and preparing environmental documents, particularly in relation to NEPA and the California Environmental Quality Act. The project the associate would be especially focused on concerned a specific habitat conservation program, and the company sought individuals who had experience in analyzing and reporting on wetlands, endangered species, water quality, and cultural resources. The job entailed conducting environmental research, evaluating potential impacts, devising measures to mitigate the impacts, and writing reports.

A large part of an environmental planner's job involves reading information, analyzing data, and writing and presenting reports. Environmental planners use computer databases and spreadsheets to determine how much projects will cost and to forecast employment, housing, transportation, or population trends. They also use computerized geographic information systems to map out land areas and to show variables in population densities in areas, as well as to create alternative land-use plans by tweaking geographic information. They work closely with planning teams, land developers, civic leaders, and public officials. They also may function in helping to resolve community disputes regarding development plans by suggesting mutually acceptable options. They may also be required to speak at civic meetings and present and defend their proposals to legislative committees and elected officials.

REQUIREMENTS
High School
Environmental planners rely on solid math, science, and communication skills in their work. Be sure to take classes in math, ecology, geology, natural sciences, environmental studies, history, political science, English, and computer software and design programs.

Postsecondary Training
Federal, state, and local governments require environmental and urban planners to have a master's degree from an accredited program in environmental or urban planning. A bachelor's degree in economics, geography, political science, or environmental design provides a solid foundation for graduate studies. According to the U.S. Department of Labor, in 2007 66 colleges offered accredited master's degree programs in planning, and 15 offered bachelor's degree programs. Many schools now offer undergraduate and graduate degree programs in resource and environmental planning and environmental studies. Graduates can specialize in such areas as land-use or code enforcement, community development and redevelopment, natural resources and environmental planning, urban planning, transportation planning, and economic planning and development.

In addition to course work in environmental planning, undergraduates also study earth sciences, architecture, economics, law, finance, health administration, and management. Environmental planners regularly use computer models and statistics in their work, so these classes as well as computer science and geographic information systems classes are recommended.

Certification or Licensing
To date, New Jersey is the only state that requires planners to be licensed. Licensure is granted to applicants who pass two exams, one that focuses on general knowledge of planning, and a second that tests knowledge of New Jersey planning laws. Michigan requires registration to use the title "community planner." Registrants must have professional work experience and pass national and state exams in order to receive the community planner title.

Certification is voluntary and can broaden an environmental planner's opportunities for work. To qualify for certification from the American Institute of Certified Planners or the National Association for Environmental Planners, for example, applicants must meet educational and professional requirements, and pass an exam.

To maintain the certified planner designation, planners must participate in ongoing professional development activities to keep their skills fresh and to stay up to date on trends, technologies, and best practices.

Other Requirements

A myriad of skills and character traits are required to adeptly and successfully handle the job of being an environmental planner. Creative and analytical thinking is a key component. Planners need to be able to incorporate numerous details into their plans and visualize the effects of their designs. Diplomacy and flexibility are called upon regularly in this type of work. Planners collaborate with various team members and clients and must be able to constructively resolve differences of opinion to keep projects moving forward as well as to keep design aspects in compliance with environmental regulations. Strong knowledge of environmental policy and laws, as well as laws specific to the projects on which they are working, is required for all levels of environmental planning. Clear, strong communication skills—both written and verbal—are also essential for day-to-day tasks, including making presentations, discussing and negotiating various aspects of projects and contracts, and instructing and managing other staff and team members. The ability to work independently and as part of a team is also intrinsic to the job at all levels.

EXPLORING

The Education section of the American Planning Association's (APA) Web site offers useful information for students interested in pursuing a career in planning. To learn more about what planning is, find listings of schools that offer degree programs in planning, and see available scholarships in this area, visit http://www.plan ning.org/education/resources/index.htm. You can also find book recommendations, upcoming conferences and events, and see if your neighborhood is included in the "2008 Great Places in America" (which also includes great streets and great public places that planners helped create), by visiting the Outreach section of APA's site.

EMPLOYERS

About 34,000 urban and regional planners were employed in the United States in 2006, according to the U.S. Department of Labor.

The majority (68 percent) worked for local governments. Many others worked in the private sector for architectural, engineering, scientific, management, and technical consulting companies. State and federal government agencies that focus on housing, transportation, or environmental protection also employ planners.

STARTING OUT

Many environmental planners get their start while in school, working part time or interning with an environmental or urban planning agency. Professional associations such as the National Association of Environmental Professionals also offer numerous resources, including networking opportunities and job listings. Environmental planners are concerned with a variety of issues, ranging from environmental and scientific, to economic, political, and ethical. Read newspapers, magazines, trade publications, and books to keep up with current events and industry trends.

ADVANCEMENT

Environmental planners can advance to become senior environmental planners, handling larger and more complex projects. With years of experience, they may become managers or directors, overseeing the work of more staff members or more departments or regions. Planners who are on staff with companies may leave the position to start their own environmental planning businesses. They may provide consulting services to other companies and take contract jobs with agencies. Another path of advancement may lead planners back to school, to teach environmental planning in colleges and universities. They may also share their knowledge by writing books and articles about the subject, and participating in speakers' panels at professional association conferences.

EARNINGS

Salaries specific to environmental planners are not included in the reports by the U.S. Bureau of Labor Statistics (BLS). The BLS does show, however, that in 2008 urban and regional planners had median annual incomes of $59,810, with the lowest paid 10 percent earning $37,960 and the top paid 10 percent earning $91,520 or more. Those working for federal government agencies averaged higher annual salaries ($85,100) than those who worked for local governments ($60,360). In 2008 legal services companies paid planners annual salaries of $82,350, while architectural, engineering, and related services paid their planners $69,090 per year. The states where urban and regional planners earned the highest incomes were the District of Columbia, Nevada, California, Illinois, and New Jersey.

WORK ENVIRONMENT

Work hours for environmental planners can be 40 hours per week or more. Their schedules will vary based on the intensity and complexity of the projects they are working on and the deadlines. Flexibility to work evenings and weekends is often required to accomplish job goals. Planners travel to meetings with clients and citizens' groups, to public hearings, and to project sites. Environmental planning work can be stressful due to a combination of deadline pressures and tight schedules, along with special interest groups that often exert political pressure regarding opinions on urban development and land-use proposals. The ability to juggle work tasks while maintaining diplomacy, tact, and professionalism is essential to succeed as an environmental planner.

OUTLOOK

Environmental planners can expect to have decent employment opportunities in the coming years as the focus on sustainable development and environmentally friendly building and design continues to grow. Planners with master's degrees, strong computer skills (especially global information software knowledge), and a proven track record of successful planning will have an advantage in the job hunt.

The U.S. Department of Labor predicts faster than average employment growth for urban and regional planners overall through 2016. State and local governments will need to provide more public services such as regulation of the environment, commercial development, transportation, housing, and land use for the growing population. Environmental planners will be needed to help create plans for communities requiring roads and sewer systems, schools and libraries, and recreation facilities. They will also be hired to help with historic preservation and redevelopment projects. The private sector, which employs about 21 percent of all urban and regional planners, is also expected to show rapid employment growth for planners.

FOR MORE INFORMATION

The APA was founded in 1978, but its roots actually date back to 1909, when the first National Conference on City Planning was held in Washington, D.C. Find membership information and other resources related to planning by visiting its Web site.

American Planning Association (APA)
1776 Massachusetts Avenue, NW, Suite 400
Washington, DC 20036-1904
Tel: 202-872-0611
http://www.planning.org

Find information on accredited urban and regional planning programs by visiting the following Web site:

Association of Collegiate Schools of Planning
6311 Mallard Trace
Tallahassee, FL 32312-1570
Tel: 850-385-2054
http://acsp.org

Founded in the mid-1970s, the NAEP offers certification programs, educational courses and seminars, regional meetings and events, and access to a career center and job postings. For further information, visit

National Association of Environmental Planners (NAEP)
PO Box 460
Collingswood, NJ 08108-0460
Tel: 856-283-7816
http://www.naep.org

Environmental Specialists

OVERVIEW

Environmental specialists are employed by federal, state, and local environmental protection agencies, as well as private-sector companies, to gather and interpret environmental data to ensure that business operations are in compliance with environmental regulations and standards. They specialize in various areas including air, water, hazardous waste, and emergency preparedness.

HISTORY

Since the 1970s, stricter environmental laws and regulations have been enacted to prevent and control pollution and improve public health. Attention has focused on the impact of greenhouse gas emissions on the ozone, and research has been done to devise new ways to regulate business practices to reduce negative effects on air, land, and water. 1970 was a pivotal year in the environmental movement: The U.S. government solidified its role in environmental protection by passing the National Environmental Policy Act in January 1970; the first Earth Day—to celebrate the planet and all living creatures—was in April 1970; and the federal government established the Environmental Protection Agency in April 1970, with a mission to safeguard the natural environment and protect human health. Concerns about protecting air and water quality, cleaning up hazardous waste sites, and curbing, if not preventing, pollution have given rise to the enactment and continual amendment of numerous federal, state, and local environmental laws. A few examples include the following:

- Federal Water Pollution Control Act of 1945 (last amended 2002)
- Solid Waste Disposal Act of 1965 (last amended 2002)
- Toxic Substances Control Act of 1976 (last amended 2002)
- Clean Air Act of 1970 (last amended 2002)
- National Climate Protection Act of 1978 (last amended 2000)
- Nuclear Waste Policy Act of 1982 (last amended 2000)
- Oil Pollution Control Act of 1990 (last amended 2000)
- Pollution Prevention Act of 1990 (last amended 2002)

Past negative and tragic events have shed light on environmental regulation problems in industrial technology and manufacturing, and raised awareness about the need to take immediate action to reverse damage and prevent future incidents. For reasons such as these, environmental specialties emerged. In 1984 the Bhopal gas tragedy at a Union Carbide pesticide plant in India killed about 25,000 people when water entered a gas tank and poisonous gases were released. More than half a million people were exposed to toxic gases and chemicals. In 1986 a different type of industrial disaster occurred that raised concerns and fears about environmental regulation of nuclear power plants. The Chernobyl nuclear disaster in the Ukraine exposed over 600,000 people to nuclear radiation, and about 336,000 people needed to be resettled in uncontaminated towns. Since then, it has been difficult to directly link illnesses and deaths to the disaster, but the World Health Organization has estimated that more than 4,000 people may have died from cancer attributed to radiation exposure from Chernobyl. The *Exxon Valdez* spill in 1989 rounded out the disaster-prone decade. When the *Valdez* tanker ran aground in Prince William Sound, Alaska, it spewed 11 million gallons of oil into the water, which killed many birds, marine mammals, and fish, and damaged the ecosystem. It's still considered one of the world's worst environmental disasters.

Since these disasters, stricter standards have been enforced to monitor business practices and procedures and prevent environmental harm and impact on human health.

Environmental specialists are often the ones who suggest stronger rules and laws regarding environmental protection. Their research and analyses, in addition to other data that is gathered, are frequently used as the basis for the introduction of new rules and regulations by legislators and policy makers, and for the tightening and subsequent amendments of currently existing policies. The profession has grown over the decades to encompass a wide variety of specialties in air, land, and water.

THE JOB

Environmental specialists work in specific areas of pollution control. Their work may focus on regulating air pollution, drinking and groundwater, surface water, hazardous waste, or solid and infectious waste. Many also specialize in training and educating people for emergency preparedness and preventing pollution. Regardless of their specialization, the core tasks remain the same: gathering environmental data and interpreting it to make sure regulatory compliance standards are met. This data is often used to create environmental policy and regulations. Specialists work for government groups such as the Environmental Protection Agency and state departments of natural resources, agriculture, or health. They also work for public utilities and private-sector firms such as management and technical consulting firms and architectural, engineering, or related services.

Environmental specialists who work in air pollution regulation spend part of their time reviewing business permits for the installation and operation of equipment, processes, and facilities that emit air pollutants. Permits that allow for installation are known as PTIs (permits to install), and permits allowing for operation are known as PTOs (permits to operate). Air pollution specialists travel to the sites to inspect business operations and facilities to make sure equipment is functioning appropriately and safely and to verify that the levels of air pollutants that the companies report they are emitting match actual emissions. If specialists determine that emissions are exceeding regulatory limits, they may issue fines and citations to the responsible parties.

Specialists who work in drinking and groundwater services inspect water treatment plants and groundwater to help prevent contamination of drinking water. They work closely with drinking and groundwater technicians to take samples of water and test it in laboratories for such contaminants as arsenic, lead and copper, microbials and disinfectant byproducts, radionuclides, and radon. They may also monitor reservoirs and underground water tank facilities. When floods or disasters occur, they monitor drinking water and groundwater for hazardous materials.

Surface water specialists test and assess rivers, ponds, streams, lakes, wetlands, and other bodies of water for toxins. They also study the plant and animal life within the waters, testing for chemical, oxygen, and nutrient levels. They make sure the federal clean water regulations are met and that the waters meet the standards for their intended uses, such as for contact recreational activities (e.g., swimming and surfing) or for noncontact activities (boating and fishing). Specialists check for pollutants from storm sewers or runoff from roads, farm fields, or construction sites; they also check for permits from wastewater treatment plants or sewage plants, and test for pollutants that may stem from these plants.

Hazardous waste specialists monitor business operations for hazardous waste. The Environmental Protection Agency (EPA) categorizes hazardous waste into the following categories: liquid wastes (from common manufacturing and industrial processes, from specific industries, and from chemical products); characteristic wastes, which exhibit ignitability, corrosivity, reactivity, or toxicity; universal wastes (such as batteries, pesticides, and mercury-containing equipment); and mixed wastes, which contain both radioactive and hazardous waste components. The EPA also describes the Waste Identification Process, which is important in identifying, characterizing, listing (as well as removing from the list) hazardous wastes. Hazardous waste specialists review permits and paperwork regarding the generation, storage, transportation, treatment, and disposal of hazardous waste. They also inspect hazardous waste sites, review records via databases and spreadsheets, and oversee hazardous waste sampling for characterization assessment. In some private-sector jobs, they may be responsible for planning, coordinating, and scheduling hazardous waste disposal. They also write reports as frequently as required, which could be weekly, monthly, or quarterly. They attend meetings with clients (known in the industry as "generators"), take training courses to keep up to date on techniques and regulations, and may be required to teach classes as well. Those who specialize in solid and infectious waste have similar responsibilities, although they deal more closely with hospitals, solid waste districts, and landfills.

Some specialists work in the area of pollution prevention, educating business owners and the general public about the ways in which they can adjust their business and domestic practices to reduce pollution, such as by reusing and recycling materials and aiming for zero landfill. They share their knowledge by speaking at community and citizen group meetings, attending business meetings and conferences, speaking at public schools and universities, creating fact sheets and print and online presentations, and writing articles and press releases for media distribution.

Training, preparing, and responding to emergencies is another important specialty within the environmental regulation field. When industrial spills and disasters occur, or if hazardous waste is discovered, quick environmental remediation is required. Environmental specialists trained in cleaning up sites are prepared for this type of work and immediately dispatched to the site to begin addressing the problems. Natural disasters also require environmental cleanup and follow-up testing to ensure safety and health. Some specialists will be sent to any part of the world where disasters have occurred to be part of international remediation teams.

REQUIREMENTS
High School
Environmental specialists work in a variety of areas, so it's a good idea while you're in high school to get a well-rounded education by taking classes in the sciences (including biology, chemistry, geology), math, history, environmental studies, English, computers, and a foreign language. The ability to analyze data and write clear, concise reports is an important part of the job, so be sure to also take classes that emphasize writing and communications.

Postsecondary Training
A bachelor's degree in earth sciences, such as biology or environmental science, is the minimum educational requirement to work as an environmental specialist. Bachelor's degree programs in environmental science include course work in data analysis and physical geography, which are needed to study pollution abatement, water resources, and ecosystem protection, restoration, and management. Students who want to specialize in the environmental or regulatory fields usually take classes in environmental legislation, hazardous waste management, fluid mechanics, hydrology, chemistry, and geologic logging (geologic data gathering).

More employers are requiring environmental scientists, including specialists, to have a master's degree in environmental science or a related natural science. Most research positions in private industry and at state and federal agencies require a master's degree, even at the entry level. For college teaching and most research positions, a doctoral degree is generally required.

Certification or Licensing

Environmental specialists may need to be certified or licensed, depending on their employer, the state in which they work, and their specialty—especially if they work in pollution that focuses on sanitation, public health, public water supplies, or sewage treatment systems. To improve their chances for finding work and to hone their skills, they can secure the qualified environmental professional and the environmental professional intern certifications from the Institute of Professional Environmental Practice (http://www.ipep.org). The Academy of Board Certified Environmental Professionals also offers the certified environmental professional (CEP) designation to environmental professionals who meet certain prerequisites (http://www.abcep.org).

Other Requirements

Patience, diplomacy, and mindfulness are all needed to succeed in this work. Environmental specialists work independently and on teams, visiting various sites, assessing data, writing reports, and making presentations. The ability to focus on the details, work with different personalities, and clearly communicate findings, both in writing and verbally, is essential. Strong computer knowledge is also critical. Students with experience in computer modeling, data analysis and integration, digital mapping, remote sensing, and geographic information systems will be well prepared to find work when they enter the job market.

EXPLORING

You can learn more about environmental specialist careers by reading magazines, journals, and books about environmental science. Another great way to get a head start is by reading lesson plans for environmental science classes and conducting your own experiments; *Environmental Science Activities Kit*, by Michael L. Roa will help with this. And the book *Visualizing Environmental Science*, by Linda R. Berg, will grab your attention with visuals, maps, charts, and illustrations, along with descriptions about different projects and areas in the world where environmental scientists have worked.

EMPLOYERS

The Bureau of Labor Statistics (BLS) reports that about 92,000 environmental scientists, including environmental specialists and hydrologists, were employed in the United States in 2006. State and local governments employ about 35 percent of all environmental scientists. About 21 percent work for management, scientific, and technical consulting firms. Architectural, engineering, and related services employ approximately 15 percent; and the federal government employs 8 percent. A small percent of environmental scientists (2 percent) are self-employed. Many others hold faculty positions at colleges and universities, but these statistics are classified under "postsecondary teachers" within the BLS reports.

STARTING OUT

Working as an intern with an environmental group is a great way to learn more about this field and to see if you enjoy the work. The American Society for Environmental History (ASEH), founded in 1977, is just one of the many professional organizations that offer numerous resources for environmental students and career seekers. Visit the ASEH's Web site (http://www.aseh.net) to learn more about volunteer and internship opportunities, find upcoming meetings and conferences, and learn more about environmental history and issues by reading the organization's journal, *Environmental History* (http://www.aseh.net/publications/environmental-history), and other publications.

ADVANCEMENT

Environmental specialists who work as researchers may advance to senior researcher or department director positions. They may also advance by pursuing advanced degrees or securing certification. Those who work for government agencies or private-sector service firms may start their own consulting businesses. Sharing knowledge with students through teaching and lecturing, and also by mentoring young people, is another form of career advancement for environmental specialists. Some specialists also research specific topics and write books and articles about their theories and findings.

EARNINGS

Environmental scientists and specialists had median annual incomes of $59,750 in 2008, according to the U.S. Department of Labor. The bottom paid 10 percent earned $36,310 per year and the top paid 10 percent had annual salaries of $102,610 or more. Those who worked for state governments averaged $70,450 per year, while scientists and specialists who worked for local governments brought home about $58,040 annually. Cities that paid the highest salaries included Milwaukee, Wisconsin; Framingham, Massachusetts; and San Jose, Sunnyvale, and Santa Clara, California. Salary.com shows that in 2009 environmental managers (whose responsibilities may closely match those of environmental specialists with more years of experience) had median annual incomes of $93,281, with salaries starting at $67,243 and ranging up to $119,988 or higher.

In addition to salary, environmental specialists may also receive benefits such as health insurance; paid vacation, holiday, and sick time; employer-paid training; tuition reimbursement; and pension and retirement benefits.

WORK ENVIRONMENT

Environmental specialists may work in a clean, well-lit office and laboratory one day, and find themselves in a dirty, smelly space the next day. Specialists conduct some of their work in unpleasant environments and can be exposed to hazardous and unsafe conditions. They follow strict safety precautions and procedures to protect themselves. They also spend some of their time traveling to urban, industrial, or rural sites to make observations and collect data and samples for laboratory testing. Depending on the sites they visit, their work may also involve some physical activity, such as climbing hills, stairs, or ladders. Specialists typically work 40 hours or more per week. They also spend time keeping up with developments in the field by reading books and trade publications, attending workshops and seminars, and participating in conferences.

OUTLOOK

Employment opportunities should be excellent for environmental scientists over the next few years. According to the U.S. Department of Labor, employment growth for environmental scientists will be much faster than the average for all occupations through 2016. Job growth will be especially strong in private-sector consulting firms. Increasing demand for environmental and water resources by the growing population will spur the need for specialists in this field. Stricter environmental laws and regulations—particularly in relation to groundwater contamination, clean air, and flood control—will also require specialists to ensure that business operations and procedures are in compliance. More work is being done in areas of environmental remediation and solution, with greater focus on minimizing waste, recovering resources, and preventing and controlling pollution. As a result, environmental specialists will be called upon to collect and analyze data and make recommendations for effective ways to improve environmental health.

FOR MORE INFORMATION

Find information about the CEP certification and other resources by visiting
The Academy of Board Certified Environmental Professionals
PO Box 42564
Towson, MD 21284-2564
Tel: 866-767-8073
Email: office@abcep.org
http://www.abcep.org

Learn more about environmental careers in air and waste management by visiting
Air & Waste Management Association
420 Fort Duquesne Boulevard
One Gateway Center, 3rd Floor
Pittsburgh, PA 15222-1435
Tel: 412-232-3444
Email: info@awma.org
http://www.awma.org

Find membership information and internship listings at
American Society for Environmental History
c/o Interdisciplinary Arts and Sciences Program
University of Washington
1900 Commerce Street
Tacoma, WA 98402-3112
Email: director@aseh.net
http://www.aseh.net

Find environmental job listings and other resources on ECO's Web site.

Environmental Careers Organization (ECO)
http://www.eco.org

For information on environmental careers and student employment opportunities with the EPA, contact

Environmental Protection Agency (EPA)
Ariel Rios Building
1200 Pennsylvania Avenue, NW
Washington, DC 20460-0001
Tel: 202-272-0167
Email: public-access@epa.gov
http://www.epa.gov

Learn more about certification requirements by visiting IPEP's Web site.

Institute of Professional Environmental Practice (IPEP)
600 Forbes Avenue
339 Fisher Hall
Pittsburgh, PA 15282-0001
Tel: 412-396-1703
Email: ipep@duq.edu
http://www.ipep.org

Find job listings and scholarship opportunities by visiting

National Ground Water Association
601 Dempsey Road
Westerville, OH 43081-8978
Tel: 800-551-7379
Email: ngwa@ngwa.org
http://www.ngwa.org

To learn more about conferences and workshops, contact

Water Environment Federation
601 Wythe Street
Alexandria, VA 22314-1994
Tel: 800-666-0206
http://www.wef.org

Environmental Technicians

QUICK FACTS

School Subjects
Biology
Chemistry

Personal Skills
Mechanical/manipulative
Technical/scientific

Work Environment
Indoors and outdoors
One location with some
travel

Minimum Education Level
Some postsecondary training

Salary Range
$25,830 to $40,230 to
$64,580+

Certification or Licensing
Required for certain positions

Outlook
Much faster than the average

OVERVIEW

Environmental technicians, also known as *pollution control technicians*, conduct tests and field investigations to obtain soil samples and other data. Their research is used by engineers, scientists, and others who help clean up, monitor, control, or prevent pollution. An environmental technician usually specializes in air, water, or soil pollution. Although work differs by employer and specialty, technicians generally collect samples for laboratory analysis with specialized instruments and equipment; monitor pollution control devices and systems, such as smokestack air "scrubbers"; and perform various other tests and investigations to evaluate pollution problems. They follow strict procedures in collecting and recording data in order to meet the requirements of environmental laws.

In general, environmental technicians do not operate the equipment and systems designed to prevent pollution or remove pollutants. Instead, they test environmental conditions. In addition, some analyze and report on their findings.

HISTORY

Stricter pollution control regulations introduced in the mid-1960s and early 1970s created a job market for environmental technicians. As regulations on industry have become more stringent, the job has grown both in importance and in scope. For centuries the biosphere (the self-regulating envelope of air, water, and land in which all life on earth exists) was generally able to scatter, break down, or adapt to all the wastes and pollution produced by people. The industrial revolution changed the biosphere drastically. Beginning in England in the 1750s, the industrial revolution caused the shift from a farming society to an industrialized society. Although it had many economic benefits, industrialization took a terrible toll on the environment. Textile manufacturing and iron processing spread through England, and coal-powered mills, machines, and factories spewed heavy black smoke into the air. Rivers and lakes became open sewers as factories dumped their wastes. By the 19th century, areas with high population density and clusters of factories were experiencing markedly higher death and disease rates than areas with little industrial development.

The industrial revolution spread all over the world, including France in the 1830s, Germany in the 1850s, the United States after the Civil War, and Russia and Asia (especially Japan) at the turn of the century. Wherever industry took hold, there were warning signs that the biosphere could not handle the resulting pollution. Smoke and smog from factories hung over large cities. Residents experienced more respiratory and other health problems. Manufacturing wastes and untreated sewage poisoned surface waters and underground sources of water, affecting water supplies and increasing disease. Wastes and pollution also seeped into the soil, damaging crops.

After World War II, the development of new synthetic materials and their resulting waste products, including plastics, pesticides, and vehicle exhausts, that are difficult to degrade (break down) worsened pollution problems. Fish and wildlife began to die because rivers and lakes were choked with chemicals and wastes. Scientists documented connections between pollution and birth defects, cancer, fertility problems, genetic damage, and many other serious problems.

Not until the mid-1960s to early 1970s did public outcry, environmental activism, and political and economic necessity force the passage of stricter pollution control laws. Federal environmental legislation mandated cleanups of existing air, water, and soil pollution and began to limit the type and amount of polluting substances that industry could release into the environment. Manufacturers were required to operate within stricter guidelines for air emissions, wastewater treatment and disposal, and other polluting activities. States and municipalities were also given increasing responsibilities for monitoring and working to reduce levels of auto, industrial, and other pollution. Out of the need to meet these new requirements, the pollution control industry was born—and with it, the job of environmental technician.

THE JOB

Environmental technicians usually specialize in one aspect of pollution control, such as water pollution, air pollution, or soil pollution. Sampling, monitoring, and testing are the major activities of the job. No matter what the specialty, environmental technicians work largely for or with government agencies that regulate pollution by industry.

Increasingly, technicians input their data into computers. Instruments used to collect water samples or monitor water sources may be highly sophisticated electronic devices. Technicians usually do not analyze the data they collect. However, they may report on what they know to scientists or engineers, either verbally or in writing.

Water pollution technicians monitor both industrial and residential discharge, such as from wastewater treatment plants. They help to determine the presence and extent of pollutants in water. They collect samples from lakes, streams, rivers, groundwater, industrial or municipal wastewater, or other sources. Samples are brought to labs, where chemical and other tests are performed. If the samples contain harmful substances, remedial (cleanup) actions will need to be taken. These technicians may also perform various field tests, such as checking the pH, oxygen, and nitrate levels of surface waters.

Some water pollution technicians set up monitoring equipment to obtain information on water flow, movement, temperature, or pressure and record readings from these devices. To trace flow patterns, they may inject dyes into the water.

Technicians have to be careful not to contaminate their samples, stray from the specific testing procedure, or otherwise do something to ruin the sample or cause faulty or misleading results.

Depending on the specific job, water pollution technicians may spend a good part of their time outdoors, in good weather and bad, aboard boats, and sometimes near unpleasant smells or potentially hazardous substances. Field sites may be in remote areas. In some cases, the technician may have to fly to a different part of the country, perhaps staying away from home for a long period of time.

Water pollution technicians play a big role in industrial wastewater discharge monitoring, treatment, and control. Nearly every manufacturing process produces wastewater, but U.S. manufacturers today are required to be more careful about what they discharge with their wastewater.

Some technicians specialize in groundwater, ocean water, or other types of natural waters. *Estuarine resource technicians*, for example, specialize in estuary waters, or coastal areas where fresh water and salt water come together. These bays, salt marshes, inlets, and other tidal water bodies support a wide variety of plant and animal life with ecologically complex relationships. They are vulnerable to destructive pollution from adjoining industries, cities and towns, and other sources. Estuarine resource technicians aid scientists in studying the resulting environmental changes. They may work in laboratories or aboard boats, or may use diving gear to collect samples directly.

Air pollution technicians collect and test air samples (for example, from chimneys of industrial manufacturing plants), record data on atmospheric conditions (such as determining levels of airborne substances from auto or industrial emissions), and supply data to scientists and engineers for further testing and analysis. In labs, air pollution technicians may help test air samples or re-create contaminants. They may use atomic absorption spectrophotometers, flame photometers, gas chromatographs, and other instruments for analyzing samples.

In the field, air pollution technicians may use rooftop sampling devices or operate mobile monitoring units or stationary trailers. The trailers may be equipped with elaborate automatic testing systems, including some of the same devices found in laboratories. Outside air is pumped into various chambers in the trailer where it is analyzed for the presence of pollutants. The results can be recorded by machine on 30-day rolls of graph paper or fed into a computer at regular intervals. Technicians set up and maintain the sampling devices, replenish the chemicals used in tests, replace worn parts, calibrate instruments, and record results. Some air pollution technicians specialize in certain pollutants or pollution sources. For example, *engine emission technicians* focus on exhaust from internal combustion engines.

Soil or land pollution technicians collect soil, silt, or mud samples and check them for contamination. Soil can become contaminated

An environmental technician collects soil from a field. The sample will be tested for environmental pollutants. *Health Protection Agency/Photo Researchers, Inc.*

when polluted water seeps into the earth, such as when liquid waste leaks from a landfill or other source into surrounding ground. Soil pollution technicians work for federal, state, and local government agencies, for private consulting firms, and elsewhere. (Some soil conservation technicians perform pollution control work.)

A position sometimes grouped with other environmental technicians is that of *noise pollution technician*. Noise pollution technicians use rooftop devices and mobile units to take readings and collect data on noise levels of factories, highways, airports, and other locations in order to determine noise exposure levels for workers or the public. Some test noise levels of construction equipment, chain saws, snow blowers, lawn mowers, or other equipment.

REQUIREMENTS
High School
In high school key courses include biology, chemistry, and physics. Conservation or ecology courses also will be useful, if offered at your school. Math classes should include at least algebra and geometry, and taking English and speech classes will help sharpen your communication skills. In addition, work on developing your computer skills while in high school, either on your own or through a class.

Postsecondary Training
Some technician positions call for a high school degree plus employer training. As environmental work becomes more technical and complex, more positions are being filled by technicians with at least an associate's degree. To meet this need, many community colleges across the country have developed appropriate programs for environmental technicians. Areas of study include environmental engineering technologies, pollution control technologies, conservation, and ecology. Courses include meteorology, toxicology, source testing, sampling, analysis, air quality management, environmental science, and statistics. Other training requirements vary by employer. Some experts advise attending school in the part of the country where you'd like to begin your career so you can start getting to know local employers before you graduate.

Certification or Licensing
Certification or licensing is required for some positions in pollution control, especially those in which sanitation, public health, a public

water supply, or a sewage treatment system is involved. For example, the Institute of Professional Environmental Practice offers the qualified environmental professional and the environmental professional intern certifications.

Other Requirements

Environmental technicians should be curious, patient, detail-oriented, and capable of following instructions. Basic manual skills are a must for collecting samples and performing similar tasks. Complex environmental regulations drive technicians' jobs; therefore, it's crucial that they are able to read and understand technical materials and to carefully follow any written guidelines for sampling or other procedures. Computer skills and the ability to read and interpret maps, charts, and diagrams are also necessary.

Technicians must make accurate and objective observations, maintain clear and complete records, and be exact in their computations. In addition, good physical conditioning is a requirement for some activities, such as climbing up smokestacks to take emission samples.

EXPLORING

To learn more about environmental jobs, visit your local library and read some technical and general-interest publications in environmental science. This might give you an idea of the technologies being used and issues being discussed in the field today. Explore the Web sites of professional associations for environmental technicians and specialists, such as the Institute of Professional Environmental Practice (http://www.ipep.org). You can also visit a municipal health department or pollution control agency in your community. Many agencies are pleased to explain their work to visitors.

School science clubs, local community groups, and naturalist clubs may help broaden your understanding of various aspects of the natural world and give you some experience. Most schools have recycling programs that enlist student help.

With the help of a teacher or career counselor, you might be able to arrange a tour of a local manufacturing plant that uses an air- or water-pollution abatement system. Many plants offer tours of their operations to the public, which can provide an excellent opportunity to see technicians at work.

As a high school student, it may be difficult to obtain summer or part-time work as a technician due to the extensive operations and safety training required for some of these jobs. However, it is worthwhile to check with a local environmental agency, nonprofit environmental organizations, or private consulting firms to learn of volunteer or paid support opportunities. Any hands-on experience you can get will be of value to a future employer.

EMPLOYERS

Approximately 37,000 environmental science and protection technicians are employed in the United States. Many jobs for environmental technicians are with the government agencies that monitor the environment, such as the Environmental Protection Agency (EPA) and the Departments of Agriculture, Energy, and Interior.

Water pollution technicians may be employed by manufacturers that produce wastewater, municipal wastewater treatment facilities, private firms hired to monitor or control pollutants in water or wastewater, and government regulatory agencies responsible for protecting water quality.

Air pollution technicians work for government agencies such as regional EPA offices. They also work for private manufacturers producing airborne pollutants, research facilities, pollution-control equipment manufacturers, and other employers.

Soil pollution technicians may work for federal or state departments of agriculture and EPA offices. They also work for private agricultural groups that monitor soil quality for pesticide levels.

Noise pollution technicians are employed by private companies and by government agencies such as OSHA (Occupational Safety and Health Administration).

STARTING OUT

Graduates of two-year environmental programs are often employed during their final term by recruiters who visit their schools. Specific opportunities will vary depending on the part of the country, the segment of the environmental industry, the specialization of the technician (air, water, or land), the economy, and other factors. Many beginning technicians find the greatest number of positions available in state or local government agencies.

Most schools provide job-hunting advice and assistance. Direct application to state or local environmental agencies, other potential employers, or employment agencies can also be a productive approach. If you hope to find employment outside your current geographic area, you may get good results by checking with professional organizations or by reading advertisements in technical journals, many of which have searchable job listings on the Internet.

ADVANCEMENT

The typical hierarchy for environmental work is technician (two years of postsecondary education or less), technologist (two years

---

 Phytoremediation

The job of the environmental technician works within the rigid laws of science, but the field also allows for some creativity in helping other professionals find solutions to pollution control. One such creative solution that environmental technicians have helped others make possible is phytoremediation.

Phytoremediation is the use of plants and trees to clean up contaminated soil and water. This solution is cost-effective (avoiding the use of expensive equipment and chemicals) as well as environmentally friendly, in some cases creating esthetically pleasing areas such as ponds and gardens. Plants can break down organic pollutants or stabilize metal contaminants by acting as filters or traps. Over time, plants absorb contaminants from the soil or water by soaking them up in their root system.

One example of how phytoremediation is succeeding is in Chernobyl (the site of a 1986 nuclear accident), where sunflowers floating on rafts with their roots dangling in the water are being used to remove the contaminants cesium 137 and strontium 90 from a pond. In the eastern United States, where acid mine drainage is a problem, government agencies encourage the planting of wetlands using the common cattail to soak up mining contaminants from streams. On a smaller scale, the Indian Creek Nature Center in Cedar Rapids, Iowa, used phytoremediation when its septic system became overloaded. The center built a wetlands area that includes attractive native plants. Waste from the center first goes to a conventional septic system, and then it flows to three basins, two of which are filled with pea gravel. Plants extend their roots down into the dirty water and filter out contaminants. The water, now clean, flows into the third basin—a pond that itself has become a popular attraction at the nature center.

or more of postsecondary training), technician manager (perhaps a technician or technologist with many years of experience), and scientist or engineer (four-year bachelor's of science degree or more, up to Ph.D. level).

In some private manufacturing or consulting firms, technician positions are used for training newly recruited professional staff. In such cases, workers with four-year degrees in engineering or physical science are likely to be promoted before those with two-year degrees. Employees of government agencies usually are organized under civil service systems that specify experience, education, and other criteria for advancement. Private industry promotions are structured differently and will depend on a variety of factors.

EARNINGS

Pay for environmental technicians varies widely, depending on the nature of the work they do, training and experience required for the work, type of employer, geographic region, and other factors. Public-sector positions tend to pay less than private-sector positions.

Earnings of environmental technicians vary significantly based on the amount of formal training and experience. According to the U.S. Department of Labor, the average annual salary for environmental science and protection technicians was $40,230 in 2008. Salaries ranged from less than $25,830 to more than $64,580. Technicians who work for local government earned mean annual salaries of $47,100 in 2008; those who were employed by state government earned $47,190. Technicians who become managers or supervisors can earn up to $50,520 per year or more. Technicians who work in private industry or who further their education to secure teaching positions can also expect to earn higher than average salaries.

No matter which area they specialize in, environmental technicians generally enjoy fringe benefits such as paid vacation, holidays and sick time, and employer-paid training. Technicians who work full time (and some who work part time) often have health insurance benefits. Technicians who are employed by the federal government may receive additional benefits, such as pension and retirement benefits.

WORK ENVIRONMENT

Conditions range from clean and pleasant indoor offices and laboratories to hot, cold, wet, smelly, noisy, or even hazardous settings outdoors. Anyone planning a career in environmental technology should realize the possibility of exposure to unpleasant or unsafe conditions at least occasionally in his or her career. Employers often can minimize these negatives through special equipment and procedures. Most laboratories and manufacturing companies have safety procedures for potentially dangerous situations.

Some jobs involve vigorous physical activity, such as handling a small boat or climbing a tall ladder. For the most part, however, technicians need only be prepared for moderate activity. Travel may be required; technicians go to urban, industrial, or rural settings for sampling.

Because their job can involve a considerable amount of repetitive work, patience and the ability to handle routine are important. Yet, particularly when environmental technicians are working in the field, they also have to be ready to use their resourcefulness and ingenuity to find the best ways of responding to new situations.

EPA Laws

As late as the 1950s, there were few environmental technicians. Laws passed in the 1960s and later created the need for professionals to monitor and regulate pollution of soil, water, and air.

The Clean Air Act, passed in 1970, is the comprehensive federal law that regulates air emissions from factories and other sources. The act sets maximum pollutant standards, applicable mainly to industry. For example, if smokestacks at a factory are found to emit pollutants beyond the maximum allowed, the government enforces sanctions, such as fines, and requires the factory to reduce emissions by installing scrubbers, changing their processes, or other solutions.

The Pollution Prevention Act, passed in 1990, focuses industry, government, and public attention on reducing the amount of pollution by making better use of raw materials. This act advocates source reduction, i.e., reducing the amount of waste or pollution produced in the first place, rather than trying to treat it after the fact. Practices encouraged include recycling, source reduction, and sustainable agriculture. For more information on the comprehensive laws that support the EPA's authority, visit the EPA's Web site (http://www.epa.gov).

OUTLOOK

Environmental technicians are expected to have excellent job opportunities in the coming years. The U.S. Department of Labor predicts job growth will be much faster than the average for all occupations through 2016. Those trained to handle increasingly complex technical demands will have the upper hand. Environmental technicians will be needed to regulate waste products; to collect air, water, and soil samples for measuring levels of pollutants; to monitor compliance with environmental regulations; and to clean up contaminated sites.

Demand will be higher in some areas of the country than others, depending on specialty; for example, air pollution technicians will be especially in demand in large cities, such as Los Angeles and New York, which face pressure to comply with national air quality standards. Amount of industrialization, stringency of state and local pollution control enforcement, health of the local economy, and other factors also will affect demand by region and specialty. Perhaps the greatest factors affecting environmental work are continued mandates for pollution control by the federal government. As long as the federal government supports pollution control, the environmental technician will be needed.

FOR MORE INFORMATION

For job listings and certification information, contact
Air & Waste Management Association
420 Fort Duquesne Boulevard
One Gateway Center, 3rd Floor
Pittsburgh, PA 15222-1435
Tel: 412-232-3444
Email: info@awma.org
http://www.awma.org

For information on the engineering field and technician certification, contact
American Society of Certified Engineering Technicians
PO Box 1536
Brandon, MS 39043-1536
Tel: 601-824-8991
http://www.ascet.org

Learn more about environmental jobs by visiting
Environmental Careers Organization
http://www.eco.org

For information on environmental careers and student employment opportunities, contact
Environmental Protection Agency
Ariel Rios Building
1200 Pennsylvania Avenue, NW
Washington, DC 20460-0001
Tel: 202-272-0167
Email: public-access@epa.gov
http://www.epa.gov

For information on certification, contact
Institute of Professional Environmental Practice
600 Forbes Avenue
339 Fisher Hall
Pittsburgh, PA 15282-0001
Tel: 412-396-1703
Email: ipep@duq.edu
http://www.ipep.org

For job listings and scholarship opportunities, contact
National Ground Water Association
601 Dempsey Road
Westerville, OH 43081-8978
Tel: 800-551-7379
Email: ngwa@ngwa.org
http://www.ngwa.org

For information on conferences and workshops, contact
Water Environment Federation
601 Wythe Street
Alexandria, VA 22314-1994
Tel: 800-666-0206
http://www.wef.org

EPA Special Agents

OVERVIEW

EPA special agents are specially trained law enforcement officers who work for the Environmental Protection Agency, helping to enforce federal environmental laws. They work in the Criminal Investigations Unit and help protect land, water, and air resources. They are authorized to carry firearms, to serve warrants, and to place known environmental violators and fugitives under arrest.

HISTORY

In the 1960s public awareness grew regarding the harm being done to the environment and living creatures by pesticides and pollution. Rachel Carson's book *Silent Spring*, published in 1962, helped raise this awareness by pointing out how chemicals were harming wildlife, particularly birds, and that these chemicals also stayed in people's bodies their entire lives. To address public concerns, in January 1970 President Richard Nixon signed the National Environmental Policy Act to establish a federal role in environmental protection. Global awareness was raised even further when the first Earth Day happened on April 22, 1970. The day was meant to celebrate clean air, land, and water, and optimism for the new spring season. Millions of people participated—with teach-ins, lectures, musical events, and more. Earth Day was a success and has since continued to be an annual, global event. On December 2, 1970, the Environmental Protection Agency (EPA) was officially open for business. It was created to bring together federal research, monitoring, standard setting, and enforcement activities into one agency, with a focus on protecting the environment. According to its Web site, the "EPA's mission is to protect human health and to safeguard the natural environment—air, water, and land—upon which life depends. For more than 30 years, the EPA has been working for a cleaner, healthier environment for the American people."

The EPA's early years were bumpy. It was initially a poorly organized operation. Four different departments that had previously existed as their own separate entities were now condensed under the singular EPA umbrella, and employees that had been transferred along with those departments had to find ways to work through the chaos. EPA administrator William D. Ruckelshaus straightened things out. The departments that folded into the EPA were:

1. Air, Solid Waste, Radiological Health, Water Hygiene, and Pesticide Tolerance functions and personnel, which had been transferred from the Department of Health, Education, and Welfare
2. Water Quality and Pesticide Label Review, which came from the Interior Department
3. Radiation Protection Standards, which came from the Atomic Energy Commission and the Federal Radiation Council
4. Pesticide Registration, which came from the Department of Agriculture

Many environmental laws—new ones as well as resurrected and reworked ones—were enacted in the 1970s, including the Marine Protection Research and Sanctuaries Act (1972), the Endangered Species Act (1973), the Wild and Scenic Rivers Act (1976), the Marine Mammal Protection Act (1972), the Deepwater Ports and Waterways Safety Act (1974), the Water Resources Planning Act (1977), the Environmental Quality Improvement Act (1970), and the Environmental Education Act (1970). There was also renewed enforcement of the Rivers and Harbors Act of 1899.

Highlights of the 1980s included the EPA helping in the cleanup of Three Mile Island (a nuclear power-plant accident in Pennsylvania) and in relocating Love Canal residents (a toxic-waste disaster in a neighborhood in Niagara Falls, New York, which caused many illnesses and diseases). The EPA pressed for and got the Superfund law passed to cleanup abandoned waste sites. It also mandated sanctions for states not meeting air standards. In the 1990s the Clean Air Act (first passed in 1970) was amended to provide further protections, particularly regarding dust and soot. In addition, the Pollution Protection Act was passed to prevent pollution before it begins. The EPA also started partnering with companies to explore and test new, voluntary approaches to environmental protection. It had also begun work on standards for cleaner cars and fuels. In the past decade, the EPA proposed the first-ever mercury emissions regulations on power plants, issued the Clean Air Non-road Diesel Rule, and became (in 2006) the first major federal agency to purchase green power equal to 100 percent of its annual electricity use.

THE JOB

EPA special agents are part of the EPA's Criminal Investigation Division (EPA CID). They are highly trained, fully authorized law enforcement officers tasked with enforcing U.S. environmental laws as well as any other federal laws in accordance with the guidelines set by the U.S. Attorney General. EPA CID special agents are men and women who bring diverse backgrounds to their jobs. They work to protect air, water, and land resources, and have statutory authority to conduct investigations, carry firearms, make arrests for any federal crime, and execute and serve any warrant.

Special agents investigate cases involving negligent, knowing, or willful violations of federal environmental law. A knowing violation means that the violator may not have known the specific environmental statutes or regulations, but acted deliberately, and the violation was not the result of an accident. A willful violation means the violator was fully aware of the statues and regulations, and still made the violation. An agent's work involves research to learn more about the possible violation and violator, interviews with people of interest, and note taking and report writing.

Other types of environmental crimes that special agents investigate include lying to the government, fraud, or conspiracy. Some examples of environmental crimes, as described on EPA's Web site, include the following:

> ❧ Clean Water Act: To avoid having to buy the chemicals needed to run the wastewater treatment unit at a metal finishing company, a plant manager instructs employees

to bypass the facility's wastewater treatment unit. By doing this, the company sends untreated wastewater directly to the sewer system, violating the permit issued by the municipal sewer authority. The plant manager is guilty of a criminal violation of the Clean Water Act.

❧ Resource Conservation and Recovery Act (RCRA): To avoid having to pay for proper treatment of its hazardous waste, the owner of a cleaning-solvents manufacturing company places at least 30 five-gallon buckets of highly flammable and caustic waste into its dumpster for disposal at a local, municipal landfill that is not authorized to receive hazardous waste. The owner of the company is guilty of a criminal violation of RCRA.

❧ Clean Air Act: The owner of an apartment complex solicits bids to remove 14,000 square feet of old ceiling tiles from the building. Three bidders inspect the building and determine that the tiles contain dangerous asbestos fibers. These three bid, pointing out that in doing the removal, they will be required to adhere to work practice standards in compliance with asbestos removal. A fourth bidder offers a cost-savings to the owner, proposing to remove the tiles without following work practice standards. The owner hires the fourth bidder on this basis and the work is done without following the work practice standards. The owner is guilty of a criminal violation of the Clean Air Act.

Other types of crimes that special agents may investigate include illegally disposing of hazardous waste; exporting hazardous waste without getting permission from the country that's receiving it; illegally discharging pollutants to a U.S. body of water; and removing and disposing of regulated asbestos-containing materials in a manner that does not comply with the law. They may also investigate the illegal importation into the United States of restricted or regulated chemicals, tampering with a drinking-water supply, mail fraud, wire fraud, conspiracy, or money laundering relating to environmental criminal activities.

EPA CID special agents may also serve on Environmental Crime Task Force Teams by coordinating their work with other law enforcement officials and environmental agencies. The mission of these task force teams is to come up with ways to improve the support of environmental-crime enforcement and to brainstorm how to prevent crime before it happens. Members of these teams collaborate

It Might Be an Environmental Violation if You See...

1. Abandoned containers or drums, especially if they're leaking or corroded, in a place where they don't seem to belong (such as in a forest or alongside a road)
2. Waterways that look like they contain foreign substances (e.g., bleach, chemicals, detergent, or a strange color), and dead fish in waterways and streams
3. Dead animals in a field or by a riverbank
4. Discolored or dying plant life
5. Water or ground that appears to have a visible sheen on it
6. Strange-looking or foul-smelling emissions in the air
7. Pipes or valves that look like they're allowing the bypass of wastewater treatment systems
8. A truck dumping materials into a sewer drain or manhole
9. A truck unloading drums at a strange hour or in an odd place

Source: Environmental Protection Agency

by sharing information and providing knowledge and support to each other.

Another part of an EPA special agent's job may involve investigating fugitives. Sometimes people who have been charged with an environmental crime or violation of the U.S. Federal Criminal Code leave the court's jurisdiction, or even the United States, to avoid prosecution and the possibility of having to serve a jail sentence. When they do this, they become fugitives from justice, and agents will work with criminal investigation teams to track them down and arrest them.

REQUIREMENTS
High School
A well-rounded education will provide a solid foundation for future work as an EPA special agent. Take classes in math, science, history, environmental studies (if offered at your school), English, a foreign

language, and computer science. Agents need to be physically fit as well, so be sure to take gym classes and make exercise a part of your regular routine.

Postsecondary Training

An undergraduate degree is usually required for EPA special agent positions. Fields of study can include business, math, science, English, communications, and psychology. Criminal justice studies are generally not required. Fluency in another language is particularly useful in this line of work, so be sure to take foreign language classes. Advanced degrees and work experience are usually required for positions of higher authority.

Other Requirements

Applicants for a position as an EPA special agent must be between 21 and 37 years old and in excellent physical condition. They must have manual dexterity to operate a firearm, and good vision in each eye (with or without correction). The job has multiple demands and can be very stressful, so emotional and mental stability is required. Special agents receive eight weeks of basic federal law enforcement and criminal investigator training at the Federal Law Enforcement Training Center in Glynco, Georgia. They also receive an additional eight weeks of training in conducting investigations of the criminal provisions of federal environmental laws. As is the case with all U.S. special agents, EPA special agents receive periodic in-service training as well as advanced training in various investigative techniques throughout their careers.

EXPLORING

The best way to learn more about the EPA and this type of work is to get a summer job with the agency. The EPA offers summer employment at its headquarters in Washington, D.C., and at regional offices and laboratories nationwide, through its Student Temporary Employment Program (STEP). To meet STEP qualifications, students must be enrolled or accepted for enrollment in an accredited high school, college, university, or technical or vocational school. They must be in good academic standing, with at least a GPA of 2.0. They must be U.S. citizens, at least 16 years of age at the time of employment, and if 16, have a work permit. To find out more, visit the Student Employment Opportunities section of the EPA's Web site (http://www.epa.gov/ohr/student/).

You can also learn more about being an EPA special agent and other law enforcement jobs by reading *Career Opportunities in Law Enforcement, Security, and Protective Services* (second edition), by Susan Echaore-McDavid; and get more detailed information about the EPA itself by reading the book *The Environmental Protection Agency: Cleaning Up America's Act (Understanding Our Government)*, by Robert W. Collin.

EMPLOYERS

The Criminal Investigation Division of the Environmental Protection Agency has 10 regional offices throughout the United States, each of which is responsible for serving several states and territories. EPA special agents may work in one of the following EPA regions:

- Region 1: New England (Connecticut, Maine, New Hampshire, Rhode Island, Vermont, and 10 tribal nations)
- Region 2: New Jersey, New York, Puerto Rico, U.S. Virgin Islands, and seven tribal nations
- Region 3: The Mid-Atlantic States (Delaware, District of Columbia, Maryland, Pennsylvania, Virginia, and West Virginia)
- Region 4: Southeast (Alabama, Florida, Georgia, Kentucky, Mississippi, North Carolina, South Carolina, Tennessee, and six tribes)
- Region 5: Illinois, Indiana, Michigan, Minnesota, Ohio, Wisconsin, and 35 tribes
- Region 6: Arkansas, Louisiana, New Mexico, Oklahoma, Texas, and 66 tribes
- Region 7: Iowa, Kansas, Missouri, Nebraska, and nine tribal nations
- Region 8: Colorado, Montana, Nebraska, South Dakota, Utah, Wyoming, and 27 tribal nations
- Region 9: Arizona, California, Hawaii, Nevada, Pacific Islands, and over 140 tribal nations
- Region 10: The Pacific Northwest (Alaska, Idaho, Oregon, Washington, and native tribes)

Each region has its own Web site within the EPA's site. Visit the Where You Live section on the contact page (http://www.epa.gov/epahome/comments3.htm), click on the area of the map where you are located, and learn more about EPA activities within your region.

STARTING OUT

In addition to the STEP program mentioned in the previous Exploring section, students can also gain firsthand experience through the EPA's Student Career Experience Program through its Office of Enforcement and Compliance Assurance. Students who meet specific qualifications can work in paid part-time, semester-length, seasonal, or summer-trainee positions that can lead to a possible staff job with the EPA. Students must have completed 640 hours of on-the-job training and received their undergraduate degree to qualify for full-time employment with the EPA.

ADVANCEMENT

With a few years of experience and proven track record, EPA special agents can advance to become *assistant special agent in charge.* The next step up is *special agent in charge,* where they are responsible for supervising agents and staff, and managing criminal investigation programs in multi-jurisdictions and across multiple regions. Special agents may also be able to move into different departments within the EPA.

EARNINGS

EPA special agents are federal government employees. The federal government usually assigns a pay system grade to each position and a level or step within each grade through the Office of Personnel Management (OPM). The OPM calls this pay-scale system the General Schedule, or GS. The GS grade level starts at 1 and goes up to 15, thus jobs are ranked GS-1 through GS-15. The steps within the 15 grades run from 1 through 10. Salaries vary depending on the grade, step, and location of the job. Lower grade levels and steps usually pay lower salaries, while higher grade levels and steps pay higher salaries. For example, in 2009 entry-level employees who started at the GS-1, Step 1/10 level earned $17,540 per year. Those at the GS-8, Step 5/10 level earned $42,019 per year. In 2009 the salary for a supervisory criminal investigator at the GS-1811 series level, and at a grade level of 14—a position requiring previous years of experience—ranged from $98,824 to $128,607. According to OPM, professional and administrative positions generally start at the GS-5 level for entry-level college graduates. Most EPA special agents start at higher level salaries, typically within the GS-5 or higher range earlier in their careers. In 2009 GS-5 employees earned annual salaries ranging from $27,026 for Step 1, to $30,630 for Step 5, to $35,135 for Step 10.

In addition to salaries, as federal government employees EPA special agents receive numerous benefits, including paid holidays, annual leave and sick leave, federal retirement plans, paid health insurance, childcare and childcare tuition assistance, eldercare, access to a fitness center, tuition assistance and student loan reimbursement, among other incentives.

WORK ENVIRONMENT

EPA special agents work in offices and have at least 40-hour workweeks. Hours will vary and will increase when cases are heating up. Some travel is required for the job. For instance, one of the requirements of an EPA supervisory criminal investigator in Atlanta, Georgia, was the ability to travel six to 10 days per month. Agents may also spend time outside to conduct investigations. When outdoors, special agents work in any type of weather, so physical fitness and endurance are important.

OUTLOOK

Environmental laws and regulations will continue to be passed, amended, and maintained. Unfortunately, there will always be people out there looking for ways to save money and hassle by evading the laws. EPA special agents will continue to be needed to help prevent and enforce environmental laws and regulations. Competition for jobs will be keen, however, as this is a niche field and there are typically more applicants than there are jobs to fill. According to the U.S. Department of Labor, while job opportunities in most local police departments will be excellent in the next few years, average employment growth is expected for law enforcement positions within state and federal agencies through 2016. Some employment growth will be attributed to agents retiring from the field or advancing to other positions within the EPA.

FOR MORE INFORMATION

Learn more about the Environmental Protection Agency Criminal Investigation Division and EPA special agent requirements by visiting

Environmental Protection Agency (EPA) (Criminal Investigation Division)
http://www.epa.gov/compliance/criminal/investigations/

Find information about EPA careers and links for job postings by visiting the Careers section of the EPA's Web site.

Environmental Protection Agency (EPA) (Careers)
http://www.epa.gov/careers/

Find Environmental Protection Agency job postings and other resources at
USAJOBS
http://www.usajobs.opm.gov/

Fish and Game Wardens

School Subjects
Biology
Earth science

Personal Skills
Helping/teaching
Leadership/management

Work Environment
Primarily outdoors
Primarily multiple locations

Minimum Education Level
Bachelor's degree

Salary Range
$18,000 to $42,290 to
$91,000

Certification or Licensing
None available

Outlook
About as fast as the average

OVERVIEW

Fish and game wardens are now widely known as *professional wildlife conservationists.* A variety of jobs fall under this category in the federal government, such as *wildlife inspectors, refuge rangers* and *refuge officers, U.S. Fish and Wildlife Service special agents,* and *federal law enforcement officers.* Job titles at the state or municipal level might include *conservation police, environmental conservation police,* or *conservation wardens.* In addition to the expansion of the job title, the job description has also grown over the years. In the past, fish and game wardens worked solely to protect wildlife. Today, in addition to that original purpose, they perform a wide variety of tasks related to resource management, public information, and law enforcement.

HISTORY

Until the late 1800s, wildlife served two major purposes: food and entertainment. Hunting and killing game (mammals, birds, or fish that are hunted noncommercially for food and/or sport) became so popular that some animal species were literally hunted to extinction. In addition to this widespread disregard for wildlife, the development of land was growing to accommodate the increase in agriculture and industrialization. Forests were being cleared, swamps drained, and rivers dammed to make way for farms and for manufacturing plants, and many animal and plant habitats were harmed or destroyed along the way.

At the turn of the 19th century, concern had grown regarding the vanishing wildlife, which led to conservation actions. The governments of the United States and other nations have since passed protective laws and set aside national parks and other reserves for wildlife. The principal agency assigned to the conservation and enhancement of animals and their habitats in this country is the U.S. Fish and Wildlife Service. An agency of the U.S. Department of the Interior, it is responsible for the scientific development of commercial fisheries and the conservation of fish and wildlife. The service, which was officially created in 1940 and with roots dating back to 1871, manages the 150 million-acre National Wildlife Refuge System. This system includes more than 550 National Wildlife Refuges, thousands of smaller wetlands, and other special management areas. It also operates 70 National Fish Hatcheries, 64 fishery resource offices, nine Fish Health Centers, seven Fish Technology Centers, and 78 ecological services field stations. The objectives of the U.S. Fish and Wildlife Service, per its Web site, are to "assist in the development and application of an environmental stewardship ethic for our society, based on ecological principles, scientific knowledge of fish and wildlife, and a sense of moral responsibility; guide the conservation, development, and management of the nation's fish and wildlife resources; and administer a national program to provide the public opportunities to understand, appreciate, and wisely use fish and wildlife resources."

THE JOB

Responsibility for conserving and protecting wildlife has deepened and grown more complex in the past decade due to environmental changes such as global warming and the proliferation of tighter environmental laws and regulations. To meet its objectives, the U.S. Fish and Wildlife Service employs many of the country's best wildlife managers, biologists, engineers, realty specialists, law enforcement agents, and others who work to save endangered and threatened species; conserve migratory birds and inland fisheries; provide expert advice to other federal agencies, industry, and foreign governments; and manage nearly 700 offices and field stations. These personnel work in every state and territory from the Arctic Ocean to the South Pacific, and from the Atlantic to the Caribbean.

Wildlife inspectors and *special agents* are jobs that evolved from fish and game wardens. Wildlife inspectors monitor the legal trade and intercept illegal importations and exportations of federally protected fish and wildlife. They examine shipping containers, live animals, wildlife products such as animal skins, and documents at points of entry to the United States. They work closely with special agents, and may seize shipments as evidence, conduct investigations, and testify in courts of law.

Special agents of the U.S. Fish and Wildlife Service are trained criminal investigators who enforce federal wildlife laws throughout the United States. They have statutory authority to carry a firearm, serve warrants, and make arrests. Special agents conduct law enforcement investigations, which may include activities such as surveillance, undercover work, and preparing cases for court. They often work with other federal, tribal, foreign, state, or local law enforcement authorities. These agents enforce traditional migratory bird regulations and investigate commercial activities involving illegal trade in protected wildlife. Some agents work at border ports to enforce federal laws protecting wildlife that enters into interstate and national commerce.

Refuge rangers or *refuge managers* are Fish and Wildlife Service professionals who work at more than 550 national refuges across the country, protecting and conserving migratory and native species of birds, mammals, fish, endangered species, and other wildlife. Many of these refuges also offer outdoor recreational opportunities and programs to educate the public about the refuges' wildlife and their habitats.

Beth Ullenberg is supervisory visitor services manager at the Minnesota Valley National Wildlife Refuge (NWR) of the U.S. Fish and Wildlife Service. "I manage a staff of park rangers who provide the public with natural resources education, public interpretive programs, hunting and fishing opportunities, wildlife observation and nature photography, and help plan special events, all on the refuge." She has been with the U.S. Fish and Wildlife Service for over 16 years, having worked previously on national refuges in Oregon and South Dakota.

The best part about her job is the diversity. "I get to do a lot of different things every day and I get to be outside!" Beth says. "I may be teaching school kids about wildlife or staffing our visitor center or creating a new hiking trail or even banding ducks!" She says that the biggest challenge is that there is always so much to do,

A fish and game warden arrests a suspect on charges of felony conspiracy in the poaching of white sturgeon. *AP Photo/Ben Margot*

and "never enough hours in the day" to accomplish everything you would like to get done.

A wide variety of professionals with diverse specialties work for the U.S Fish and Wildlife Service, including *veterinary scientists, ecologists, botanists, engineers, foresters, chemists, hydrologists, land surveyors, architects, landscape architects, statisticians, library scientists, archaeologists, educators,* and *guidance counselors.* The Fish and Wildlife Service also hires administrators and business managers, realty specialists, appraisers, assessors, contract specialists, purchasing agents, budget analysts, financial managers, computer specialists and programmers, human resources professionals, and public affairs specialists. Technical, clerical, and trades and crafts positions are also available.

REQUIREMENTS

If you're serious about pursuing a career as a wildlife conservationist, Beth Ullenberg advises you to "stay in school and get a college education" and "be willing to work seasonal summer jobs and even volunteer to gain experience."

High School

Take courses in biology and other science subjects, geography, mathematics, social studies, and physical education. Also look for cooperative programs that are available at some high schools and colleges. These programs allow you to study as well as work in programs at refuges and other facilities—and in some cases, get paid for some of the hours you work at the facility.

Postsecondary Training

A bachelor's degree or three years of work-related experience is required for all positions within this category. Higher positions require at least one year of graduate studies; as you move up the scale to increasingly professional positions, master's or even doctoral degrees become mandatory.

Specialized positions require advanced education or training. For example, all biology-related positions require a bachelor's degree in biology or natural resources management, or a combination of education and experience equivalent to a degree that includes an appropriate number of semester hours in biological science. Visit http://www.fws.gov/jobs/ for an overview of educational requirements for various positions in the service.

Most positions offer additional on-the-job training. Natural resource managers and related professionals receive training at the National Conservation Training Center in Shepherdstown, West Virginia. Special agents are given 18 weeks of formal training in criminal investigative and wildlife law enforcement techniques at the Federal Law Enforcement Training Center in Glynco, Georgia. In addition, the service typically requires its employees to receive 40 hours of training each year.

Other Requirements

Some positions have physical fitness and ability requirements, so you must undergo a battery of physical tests. To qualify for a special agent position, you must meet strict medical, physical, and psychological requirements. You must also participate in mandatory drug testing and psychological screening programs.

Only the most highly qualified candidates will be interviewed for special agent positions. Those chosen undergo extensive background investigations to determine suitability for appointment. All special agent appointees must be citizens of the United States and between 21 and 37 years of age when entering. Additionally, you must sign a mobility agreement, which indicates a willingness to accept reassignment to any location in the future.

Fish and game wardens don't just work with fish and game. They spend a lot of time working with other officials and with members of the general public. Therefore, to succeed in this work, you must have good communication skills and enjoy working with people as much as caring for animals.

EXPLORING

A great way to get firsthand experience in this field is to volunteer or get an internship with a fish and wildlife facility. The ideal would be to volunteer for the U.S. Fish and Wildlife Service, but you can also gain valuable experience by serving with other environmental organizations. Visit the Web sites of the organizations that interest you most and check their volunteer sections for available opportunities. College students—and even students at select high schools—can apply for formal internships with various wildlife agencies. Internships usually provide high school or college credit, and some even pay a small stipend.

Beth Ullenberg also points out that you can gain a deeper appreciation for wildlife conservation and the people behind the movement by reading books such as Aldo Leopold's *A Sand County Almanac* and Rachel Carson's *Silent Spring*, as well as books and articles written by Teddy Roosevelt, John Muir, or Gifford Pinchot. (You will find some specific recommendations in the Further Resources section at the end of this volume.) And naturally, get outdoors as much as you can. See if your family can plan some outdoor trips. When she was growing up, Beth got an early introduction to outdoor experiences through the Girl Scouts, and even earlier experience from fishing trips with her family.

EMPLOYERS

Approximately 7,500 men and women with diverse skills and backgrounds work for the U.S. Fish and Wildlife Service. Numerous jobs are also found with other agencies of the Department of the Interior, such as the National Park Service. Individual states also have positions in this area. To learn more about available jobs and volunteer opportunities, contact your local state government, especially the state's park association.

STARTING OUT

The U.S. Fish and Wildlife Service fills jobs in various ways, including promoting or reassigning current employees, transferring employees from other federal agencies, rehiring former federal employees, or hiring applicants from outside the federal service. Many professional wildlife conservationists get their first taste of the field through a summer job. Applications for summer positions must be submitted during a specified period—usually sometime between January and April of each year. The number and types of temporary positions vary from year to year. Contact the regional office nearest you to learn about current opportunities.

For information about specific Fish and Wildlife Service job openings, contact the Office of Personnel Management (http://www. opm.gov) and locate an office near where you live. Another great resource for job listings is USAJOBS (http://www.usajobs.opm. gov), a job bank for the U.S. government.

ADVANCEMENT

The ability to relocate increases the odds for advancement in this field. Although professional wildlife conservationists can be promoted within their own facility, relocation opens up the possibility of taking a higher position whenever one opens up at any U.S. Fish and Wildlife Service location around the country.

EARNINGS

U.S. Fish and Wildlife Service employees are federally employed workers, and therefore earn salaries as prescribed by law. Service employees are classified either as General Schedule (GS) or as Wage Grade (WG). General Schedule employees—the professional, technical, administrative, and clerical workers—receive annual salaries based on their GS grades (1 through 15). GS-5 salaries in 2008 ranged from $29,656 to $38,641. GS-7 salaries ranged from $33,057 to $42,290. GS-9 salaries ranged from $44,934 to $58,549. There are some areas in the United States that have an additional geographic locality pay.

Generally, salaries at the U.S. Fish and Wildlife Service range from $18,000 up to $91,000 for more advanced positions. Law enforcement positions, especially special agents, receive higher salaries because of the danger inherent in their jobs.

WORK ENVIRONMENT

Because of the variety of positions and specialties within the wildlife conservation field, the work environment varies substantially. Wildlife inspectors, conservation police, or special agents generally

Educational Qualifications for Federal Wildlife Inspectors

GS-5: Four-year course of study above high school, leading to a bachelor's degree or three years of work-related experience, one year of which was at least equivalent to GS-4.
GS-7: One full academic year of graduate-level education or law school or superior academic achievement, or one year of specialized experience at least equivalent to GS-5.
GS-9: Two full academic years of graduate-level education or master's, LL.B., or JD, or one year of specialized experience at least equivalent to GS-7.

spend a great deal of time outdoors, sometimes in remote areas, perhaps pursuing wildlife criminals. Yet they also need to spend time indoors preparing detailed reports of their investigations and seeking additional information through Internet research.

Refuge rangers and managers also work indoors and outdoors. Biologists spend time both indoors and outdoors, as their particular job dictates. All of these employees, however, will have a passion for the land and animal life, a dedication to preserving our environment, and the desire to make a difference in effecting positive changes. It can be very rewarding work in terms of personal satisfaction and sense of accomplishment. Job hours vary, and can range from dawn to dusk, 9-to-5, and, depending on the job, can include evenings and weekends.

OUTLOOK

Government jobs depend on the political climate and the views of the current administration at the federal, national, and local levels. As awareness and concern about the environment continues to grow, however, professional wildlife conservationists will be needed to protect wildlife and habitats. "Americans, [now] more than ever, realize the importance of protecting, conserving, and valuing our natural world," Beth Ullenberg says. "They are more willing to conserve and support what they love. I think the future looks great!"

FOR MORE INFORMATION

To learn more about the wildlife conservation profession and related employment opportunities, contact the following organizations:

U.S. Fish and Wildlife Service
Department of the Interior
1849 C Street, NW
Washington, DC 20240-0001
Tel: 800-344-9453
http://www.fws.gov

U.S. National Park Service
Department of the Interior
1849 C Street, NW
Washington, DC 20240-0001
Tel: 202-208-6843
http://www.nps.gov

Hazardous Waste Management Specialists

OVERVIEW

The title *hazardous waste management specialist* encompasses a group of people who do one or more of the following: identify hazardous waste, ensure safe handling and disposal, and work to reduce the generation of hazardous waste. Because their duties vary so widely, hazardous waste management specialists may work for a number of different employers, from producers of hazardous waste such as industry, hospitals, and utilities to government agencies who monitor these producers. They may also work for the solid waste or public health departments of local governments. There are about 39,000 hazardous materials removal workers employed in the United States.

HISTORY

Today, hazardous waste management specialists oversee the handling of hundreds of substances the government identifies as hazardous to human health or the environment. In the past, this was not always the case. Prior to World War II, hazardous waste consisted of pesticides, which were under the regulation of the Food and Drug Administration, as well as by-products from a few industrial processes. Scientists and engineers who worked for the U.S. Food and Drug Administration or private industry monitored the disposal of these wastes to the minimal extent they were required to do so. Before the boom of environmental awareness and concern in the 1960s, these wastes were handled much like regular garbage, dumped directly into open waterways, buried in landfills, and stored or buried in 55-gallon drums at the industrial site.

With the emergence of the nuclear age came a new waste that no one seemed to know how to handle: radioactive waste. This waste presented unique challenges because of its insidious nature; it is generally colorless, odorless and remains hazardous for hundreds of years. Government scientists and engineers were the first to work on proper disposal with utilities that produced such waste (nuclear power plants). Today, hazardous waste management specialists work with these professionals on the handling of radioactive waste.

Postwar America also saw the beginnings of widespread use of synthetic materials. As one advertisement from the 1950s put it, America could enjoy "better living through chemistry." Unfortunately, this improvement also had a darker side. The tons of chemical wastes that chemical industries produced, in addition to some of the products themselves, were to have adverse and long-lasting effects on human health and the environment that no one foresaw. Crude oil gushing from a Union Oil Company's platform covered beaches in Santa Barbara in early 1969; only five months later the Cuyahoga River in Ohio caught fire. Public outrage directed at environmental disasters such as these signaled the end of such cavalier practices.

During the flurry of environmentally directed legislation in the 1970s, hazardous waste was not considered different from other types of pollution. The Resource Conservation and Recovery Act of 1976 gave the fledgling Environmental Protection Agency (EPA) power to assign permits for waste production and disposal, to track waste, to inspect facilities, and to fine offenders for noncompliance. That same year, the Toxic Substance Control Act forced manufacturers to submit formal notifications before they started commercially producing substances that could be toxic. Four criteria determine whether waste is hazardous: toxicity, ignitability, corrosivity, and reactivity.

Most people thought this spate of environmental legislation would cover all aspects of hazardous substance management. The Love Canal disaster proved otherwise. In 1978 residents in the Love Canal area, a neighborhood in Niagara Falls, New York, suffered a variety of sudden and unexplained illnesses and diseases, which triggered an investigation that uncovered 21,900 tons of chemical wastes buried in 55-gallon drums that had leaked into basements of houses and the local public school. The resulting publicity led to the discovery of thousands of similar sites throughout the United States. The Comprehensive Environmental Response, Compensation, and Liability Act of 1980 (CERCLA) was the political response to the furor surrounding these environmental crises.

CERCLA, or Superfund, as it came to be known, is a government fund that selects and pays for cleanup of abandoned, inoperative contaminated sites. Superfund also monitors new spills. Superfund established a National Priorities List of thousands of the worst sites, giving a budget and a timeline for completion of cleanup at these sites. In 1985, after a lukewarm beginning, Superfund was strengthened by the Superfund Amendment and Reauthorization Act (SARA). SARA expanded the environmental cleanup budget, allowed for civil suits against violators of the acts, and gave the EPA standards and deadlines to meet. Superfund undergoes constant review and evolution; some companies hire individuals whose job consists solely of tracking Superfund and associated legislative changes.

Superfund is only one example of how opportunities have grown for people who specialize in the handling of hazardous waste. The evolution of environmental awareness and stricter environmental regulations and laws have created jobs for people who can handle a variety of hazardous wastes, including leachate (liquid that leaches) from municipal landfills, gases emitted from industrial smokestacks, and chemicals buried years ago all over the United States.

THE JOB

Management of hazardous waste in the United States is handled in a variety of ways. Hazardous waste specialists are specially educated and trained to work anywhere along the continuum of hazardous waste management, strategizing and engineering ways to prevent spills or contamination before they happen, helping to control them when they do, identifying contaminated sites that have existed for years, and managing and overseeing cleanup and disposal of hazardous waste to meet environmental laws and regulations.

Another title hazardous waste management specialists may have is hazardous waste management engineer. In this job, engineers are responsible for regulating different engineering aspects of hazardous waste facilities, including combustion tanks, units, and container

Top Hazardous Substances

The Agency for Toxic Substances and Diseases Registry (ATSDR) is a federal public health agency of the U.S. Department of Health and Human Services. The ATSDR provides information to the general public and hazardous waste management specialists and other professionals about hazardous waste materials and instructs in how to handle them. In 2009 the most-viewed toxic materials, according to the ATSDR Web site, were the following:

1. Aluminum
2. Ammonia
3. Arsenic
4. Asbestos
5. Benzene
6. Cadmium
7. Chromium
8. DDT, DDE, and DDD
9. Formaldehyde
10. Lead
11. Mercury
12. Polychlorinated Biphenyls (PCBs)
13. Polycyclic Aromatic Hydrocarbons (PAHs)
14. Toluene
15. Trichloroethylene (TCE)

You can learn more about these substances and why they are dangerous by asking a science teacher, doing online research, or looking for related books in your local library.

Source: http://www.atsdr.cdc.gov

storage areas. They make sure that the combustion of hazardous wastes are in compliance with local, state, and federal environmental laws. Waste management engineers design, evaluate, and operate solid wastes storage, collection, and disposal systems, which may reduce the volume of waste by compaction, solidification, or incineration.

Cleaning up a contaminated site is a complicated task that needs to be carefully planned and documented. It's a process that may take several months or even years, and a bureaucratic process must be followed. An example of steps a hazardous waste management specialist may be involved in before any cleanup proceeds includes: 1) identification of the hazardous substance and testing to gauge the extent of contamination; 2) search for or negotiation with parties responsible for the contamination; 3) writing of a plan of how best to clean up the site and how much it may cost; 4) waiting for several months or longer for approval and funding to cleanup the site; and 5) public hearings to notify how, why, and when the cleanup will be done.

In the past, and over the course of many years, hazardous waste was simply dumped anywhere. As a result, contaminated sites exist everywhere. Before hazardous waste laws such as SARA and Superfund were passed, for example, a paint manufacturer might have innocently (and legally) dumped mounds of garbage containing toxic substances into a nearby field. Today, that dump may be leaking hazardous substances into the surrounding groundwater, which nearby communities use for drinking water. Specialists study the site and determine what hazardous substances are involved, how bad the damage is, and what can be done to remove the waste and restore the site. They suggest strategies for the cleanup within legal, economic, and other constraints. They organize and manage hazardous waste teams, and oversee the work of all personnel involved in the cleanup project, including technicians (who do the sampling, monitoring, and testing at suspect sites). Once the cleanup is underway, teams of specialists help ensure the waste is removed and the site properly restored.

Specialists who work for emergency response companies help stop or control accidental spills and leaks of hazardous waste, such as those that can occur when a tank truck containing gasoline is involved in an accident. Specialists working for hospitals or other producers of medical wastes help determine how to safely dispose of such wastes. Those working for research institutes or other small generators of radioactive materials advise employers about handling or storing materials.

Government-employed hazardous waste management specialists often perform general surveys of past and ongoing projects, assemble comparative cost analyses of different remedial procedures, and make recommendations for the regulation of new

A hazardous waste management specialist working for the Environmental Protection Agency tests samples from wastewater treatment plants and groundwater for pharmaceutical contaminates. *Andrew Holbrooke/Corbis*

hazardous wastes. Government hazardous waste management specialists make detailed analyses of hazardous waste sites, known as Remedial Investigation and Feasibility Studies. Using data provided by technicians and other support personnel, these hazardous waste specialists weigh economic, environmental, legal, political, and social factors and devise a remediation (cleanup) plan that best suits a particular site. Some help develop hazardous waste management laws.

Other specialists work in pollution control and risk assessment for private companies. They help hazardous waste-producing firms limit their waste output, decrease the likelihood of emergency situations, maintain compliance with federal regulations, and even modify their processes to eliminate hazardous waste altogether. Hazardous waste management specialists might also help develop processes that utilize potential waste.

REQUIREMENTS
High School
High school students interested in preparing for careers as hazardous waste management specialists need to be strong in chemistry and other sciences such as biology and geology. English and other communication classes will help aspiring specialists in college and beyond.

Postsecondary Training
Educational requirements will vary by employer, but in general, most organizations prefer to hire hazardous waste management specialists who have, at minimum, an undergraduate degree in environmental resource management, chemistry, geology, ecology, or engineering. Some hazardous waste management engineer positions may require bachelor's or masters degrees in nuclear engineering. Areas of expertise such as hydrology or subsurface hydrology may require a master's or doctoral degree. Course work in business management and administration is also helpful.

Certification or Licensing
Certification available to specialists is not universally recognized, and requirements for certification vary not only from state to state, but also region to region and year to year. Hazardous waste management professionals can gain one or more of the following: environmental health-related certifications from the National Environmental Health Association (NEHA): registered environmental

health specialist/registered sanitarian, certified environmental health technician, registered hazardous substances professional, registered hazardous substances specialist, registered environmental technician (RET), and the NEHA Radon Proficiency Program. Contact the association for more information on these certifications. Additionally, some employers pay for workshops run in-house by the NEHA and other associations, such as the Occupational Safety and Health Administration (OSHA), to update their employees on such topics as emergency response, Superfund regulations, and emerging technologies.

The certified hazardous materials manager designation is also available from the Institute of Hazardous Materials Management. Applicants must satisfy educational requirements and pass a multiple-choice examination. Certification must be renewed every five years. Although certification is not required, it lends weight to recommendations made by government-employed specialists and generally enhances a specialist's credibility.

Other Requirements

The relative newness of this field, its dependence on political support, the varied nature of its duties, and its changing regulations and technologies all require a large degree of flexibility. The ability to take into consideration the many economic, environmental, legal, and social aspects of each project is key, as are thoroughness and patience in completing the necessary work. Prospective employers look for job candidates with excellent communication skills, no matter what their specialty, because this position is so reliant on the shared information of numerous professionals.

EXPLORING

Those who would like to explore avenues of hazardous waste management can get involved in local chapters of citizen watchdog groups and become familiar with nearby Superfund sites. What is being done at those sites? Who is responsible for the cleanup? What effect does the site have on the surrounding community? The Center for Health, Environment and Justice, founded by Love Canal resident Lois Marie Gibbs, may be able to provide information about current concerns of citizens (see listing at the end of this article). A book written by Gibbs, *Love Canal: My Story*, details illnesses suffered by Love Canal residents and their frustration at difficulty in finding someone to take responsibility for the mess. *Love Canal: My Story* illustrates how the job of hazardous waste management specialist can make a difference in citizens' lives.

Additionally, understanding the problems of hazardous waste management and the controversy surrounding some of the limitations of Superfund provide a more detailed picture of the specialist's job. There are numerous magazines published on hazardous waste management, including those addressing the different waste generators and involved professionals—for example, chemical manufacturers, oil industry representatives, engineers, and conservationists. A few publications are *Waste Management World* (http://www.waste-management-world.com), *Journal of Environmental Quality* (http://jeq.scijournals.org), and *Journal of Natural Resources and Life Sciences Education* (http://www.jnrlse.org). Outreach programs sponsored by the Army Corps of Engineers offer presentations to high schools in some areas and may be arranged with the help of science departments and career services office staff members. Hazardous waste sites are listed on the EPA's National Priorities List Web site, at http://www.epa.gov/superfund/sites/npl/. Visit the site to learn more about existing and new sites, find out how and why they are added to the list, and follow the cleanup progress.

EMPLOYERS

Hazardous waste management specialists have opportunities with many types of employers. Federal, state, and local governments use hazardous waste management specialists in a variety of roles. On the local level, a hazardous waste management specialist may work within the public health, wastewater treatment, or municipal solid waste department enforcing local regulations and overseeing disposal of hazardous waste. Hazardous waste management specialists employed by the federal government generally have a regulatory role; they oversee the cleanup of past contamination and ensure subsequent contaminations don't occur by monitoring those who generate waste. Hazardous waste professionals in government tend to have health and safety backgrounds. In the private sector, some specialists work for several companies as independent consultants. Other specialists are employed by citizen groups and environmental organizations to provide expertise on environmental and safety hazards that may not warrant Superfund attention but still concern citizens who may be affected by them.

STARTING OUT

Employers in this field prefer hazardous waste management applicants with hands-on experience. Volunteering is one good way to acquire this experience and gauge the field to find a suitable niche. Internships are available through local nonprofit groups and the EPA, among other organizations. A good way to start is by working as a technician intern—helping to run tests, prepare samples, and compile data. Internships may pay minimal salaries, but they are a good way to gain exposure to the field and learn useful skills. Recent graduates and working professionals find jobs through trade association advertisements and on the Internet. Openings with government agencies can be found on the Web page of the Office of Personnel Management (http://www.usa-jobs.opm.gov).

Those who are still in school can start building a background now by attending local public meetings concerning hazardous waste. Read your local newspaper or visit the Web site of your city hall or county government to find out what the local issues are and learn about upcoming events. Citizen action groups that advocate environmental awareness are another good place to learn what the issues are in your area and find volunteer opportunities. You can also learn more about the field by visiting the Web sites of professional associations such as the Dangerous Goods Advisory Council (contact information is located at the end of this article).

ADVANCEMENT

To advance, hazardous waste management specialists need to be proficient in several aspects of hazardous waste management and able to handle an entire hazardous waste site or group of similar sites. This involves supervising technicians and support personnel, and collaborating with other specialists, engineers, and laboratory chemists, as well as being the party responsible for reporting to regulatory agencies. Other specialists may find positions in public relations fields or higher management levels. Still others may seek further formal education and advance upon attainment of advanced degrees. They may also write and teach about the topic. The field of hazardous waste management is a diverse one, and after specialists have a few years of work experience, the range of specialties available will become more evident.

EARNINGS

CBsalary.com, a service of Career Builder, reports that in 2009 waste management engineers had median annual incomes of $88,086, with salaries starting at $59,741 and ranging up to $112,445 or higher.

Specialists in the public and private sectors also enjoy benefits such as full health plans, vacation time, and subsidized travel arrangements. Employer-paid training is a common benefit in this field, as regulations and technology are constantly evolving and employers want specialists who are up to date.

WORK ENVIRONMENT

The complexity of regulations often makes remediation work painstakingly slow, but it also provides a measure of job security. High-publicity sites may bring considerable political and social pressure to bear on those responsible for their cleanup, especially if work appears to be moving very slowly. Competition for lucrative contracts can be fierce, and considerable effort must be made by employer and employee alike to stay abreast of changing technologies and legislation in order to be at the cutting edge of the field. The job of a specialist may require on-site exposure to hazardous wastes, and protective clothing that can hamper work efforts is often necessary. On the other end of the spectrum, there is always paperwork waiting to be completed back at the office. However, individuals in this field report a sense of accomplishment, and satisfaction in the field is extremely high. For some, the new developments that are a major part of the job provide welcome change and challenges.

OUTLOOK

The U.S. Department of Labor predicts that employment of these workers will grow about as fast as the average for all occupations through 2016. Hazardous waste management specialists with advanced education degrees, specific technical skills and knowledge, and success in past cleanup and remediation projects will have the best opportunities to find work. As with some other highly skilled environmental professions, hazardous waste management is currently suffering from a lack of qualified professionals. The sheer enormity of the hazardous waste problem, with at least 40,000 known sites and more expected to be identified in the near future,

Get the Lead Out

Hazardous waste management specialists should be familiar with a variety of wastes classified as hazardous and know their potential effects on humans and the environment. Lead, for example, can be found in air, water, dust, and soil. Lead in the air attaches to dust. Lead stays in the soil for many years. A naturally occurring substance, lead is more abundant than other hazardous wastes.

Humans can be exposed to lead from breathing air, drinking water, or ingesting soil or foods that contain lead. Almost all of the lead in the lungs enters the blood and moves to other parts of the body. Regardless of how lead enters your body, most of it is stored in bone. The effects of lead once it is in the body are the same no matter how it entered the body. Pregnant women and unborn children are especially at risk. In pregnant women, lead can be carried to the unborn child and cause premature birth and low birth weight. Young children are at risk because their bodies are more sensitive to its effects. Lead exposure has been shown to decrease intelligence scores, stunt growth, and cause hearing problems. Children are also more susceptible because they are more apt to ingest lead-tainted soil by putting dirty toys or even dirt in their mouths. To help protect the public, the government has passed laws that require manufacturers to make paint with lower lead concentrations and states to test drinking water in schools.

ensures that there will be cleanup jobs available as long as funding is available. An environmental careers survey recorded in the *Engineering News Record* cautions, "Though there's still a lot of hazardous waste to clean up, it's anyone's guess as to when it will be done."

In the years to come the trend in the hazardous waste management industry will move from a focus on waste removal, neutralization, and disposal, to a mission that revolves around waste prevention. Keeping track of trends in the field while still in school will enable you to tailor your course work to the anticipated needs of the future job market.

FOR MORE INFORMATION

For information on hazardous waste management training and two-year degree programs, contact

Advanced Technology Environmental Energy Center
500 Belmont Road
Bettendorf, IA 52722-5649
Tel: 563-441-4090
http://www.ateec.org/profdev/tribal/applications.htm

The following is a national grassroots organization founded by Lois Marie Gibbs and other Love Canal activists that offers publications on environmental health and community organization:

Center for Health, Environment and Justice
PO Box 6806
Falls Church, VA 22040-6806
Tel: 703-237-2249
Email: chej@chej.org
http://www.chej.org

Find information about workshops, conferences, and membership by visiting

Dangerous Goods Advisory Council
1100 H Street, NW, Suite 740
Washington, DC 20005-5476
Tel: 202-289-4550
Email: info@dgac.org
http://www.dgac.org

For information on certification, contact

Institute of Hazardous Materials Management
11900 Parklawn Drive, Suite 450
Rockville, MD 20852-2624
Tel: 301-984-8969
Email: ihmminfo@ihmm.org
http://www.ihmm.org

The following association provides certification for hazardous waste specialists:

National Environmental Health Association
720 South Colorado Boulevard, Suite 1000-N
Denver, CO 80246-1926

Tel: 303-756-9090
Email: staff@neha.org
http://www.neha.org

This organization provides information about safety and health in the workplace.

Occupational Safety & Health Administration
200 Constitution Avenue, NW
Washington, DC 20210-0001
http://osha.gov

The following is a branch of the military that employs engineering professionals in hazardous waste management projects such as Superfund remediation sites:

U.S. Army Corps of Engineers
441 G Street, NW
Washington, DC 20314-1000
Tel: 202-761-0011
Email: hq-publicaffairs@usace.army.mil
http://www.usace.army.mil

Hazardous Waste Management Technicians

QUICK FACTS

School Subjects
Biology
Chemistry

Personal Skills
Following instructions
Technical/scientific

Work Environment
Indoors and outdoors
Primarily multiple locations

Minimum Education Level
Associate's degree

Salary Range
$23,740 to $37,310 to $63,260

Certification or Licensing
Voluntary

Outlook
About as fast as the average

OVERVIEW

Hazardous waste management technicians are part of a team that identifies hazardous waste sites and remediates, or cleans up, any waste present. In many cases, they assist hazardous waste management specialists, who are more highly educated and tend to work on long-term planning and strategy. Technicians do on-site work like taking samples of contaminated soil or water; some work on emergency response teams that handle sites immediately after accidents involving hazardous waste. These technicians also do a lot of laboratory work, testing the samples they have taken and compiling and analyzing the results.

HISTORY

The job of hazardous waste management technician is one of the by-products of a booming hazardous waste management industry.

Before the latter half of the 20th century, little was known about the harmful effects that years of seemingly innocuous waste disposal had on the environment. The major sources of what is now considered hazardous waste before World War II were pesticides and fertilizer, under regulation by the Food and Drug Administration, and incidental products from a certain few industrial processes. In the postwar era, a nation now accustomed to the idea of big science in their everyday lives enjoyed the products of war-year discoveries that were then finding applications in the home, like petroleum-based plastics. The nuclear age also ushered in the chemical age, and hazardous wastes were being produced at an alarming rate. Concern for the havoc that was being wreaked on the environment was heightened by well-publicized disasters like an oil spill off the coast of California in the late 1960s.

The environmental legislation that this concern spawned did not delineate special regulations for hazardous waste at first. Under the requirements of the Clean Air Act, enacted in 1963, screens and scrubbers cleaned hazardous wastes from emissions before they became airborne. Similarly, the Clean Water Act, which was passed in 1972, created standards for municipal water and wastewater treatment plants that simply filtered hazardous waste from water supplies along with other solid wastes. The hazardous material that was left from these early environmental efforts was then simply dumped at regular landfills or burned, releasing toxic ash and residual hazardous material. In other words, whatever good was done by capturing these wastes in the first place was undone by the disposal methods that never treated the hazardous part of the waste.

This began to change in the mid-1970s, when the EPA was given power by a succession of acts to monitor and control the production of hazardous waste. In 1980 a national panic was ignited by the discovery of hazardous chemical seepage in a housing development in Love Canal, New York. This shocking development, the threat to families and communities everywhere who were ignorant of the chemical danger that might surround them, made the problem of hazardous waste suddenly very real for the average American. In response to this, the Comprehensive Environmental Response, Compensation, and Liability Act (CERCLA) was passed to address the problems of hazardous waste in general and specifically targeted closed or abandoned dumps across the nation. CERCLA, known as Superfund because of the billions of dollars allotted to this enormous task, and the 1986 Superfund Amendment and Reauthorization Act (SARA) set the standards and procedures for safe hazardous waste disposal that have created the entire hazardous waste industry. Superfund sites on the National Priorities List are those hazardous waste sites that have been determined the most threatening. There are approximately 11,300 on this list out of an estimated 40,000 hazardous waste sites nationwide. Site cleanups are lengthy processes, involving years, millions of dollars, and complex legislation that steadily changes from year to year, region to region, and site to site.

THE JOB

Hazardous waste management technicians are trained to safely contain and remove highly toxic or volatile materials. Broadly defined, a hazardous waste is any substance that threatens human health or the environment. Specifically, as defined by the Occupational Safety and Health Administration, hazardous waste is "a contaminated chemical or by-product of a production process that no longer serves its purpose and needs to be disposed of in accordance with the Environmental Protection Agency. This could include small amounts of chemicals such as parts washing solvents in a machine shop, or large amounts of construction by-products."

Some hazardous waste management technicians respond to emergency situations, such as petroleum or chemical spills. Other hazardous waste management technicians clean up devastating industrial messes—ugly reminders of a time when our country did not monitor environmental contamination as closely as it does today. Such sites are specifically targeted for cleanup by the federal government under the Comprehensive Environmental Response, Compensation, and Liability Act (CERCLA) of 1980, also known as Superfund.

Since many of the worst Superfund sites have been cleaned up, a larger number of hazardous waste management technicians are involved in lower priority cleanups. Many are cleaning up previously abandoned industrial sites, called brownfields, so that the land can once again be used. These sites do not pose an immediate threat to human health or the environment. In addition to helping clean up these kinds of sites, hazardous waste management technicians may identify, categorize, and dispose of hazardous waste, or help in efforts to lower the amount of hazardous waste produced in the first place. They also assist in other types of cleanup and pollution prevention efforts, including routine monitoring of air, soil, and water to make sure hazardous substances are within acceptable limits.

Nearly every industry produces hazardous waste, from food, textiles, metals, petroleum, plastics, and paper manufacturing to dry cleaning services, printing, and more. Chemical and petroleum companies are significant sources of hazardous waste. For example, one common hazardous waste is benzene, a component in fuel that has been identified as a carcinogen. Tanks of fuel around a gas station can leak, and substances from the fuel, including benzene, can seep into the ground and contaminate groundwater, which people then drink. Other hazardous wastes include solvents used

Hazardous waste management technicians adjust pipes at a nuclear reservation waste treatment plant. *AP Photo/Jackie Johnston, File*

in paint, manufacturing, and service operations such as dry cleaners. Manufacturing processes also produce certain metals that are hazardous.

The federal government is also a leading generator of hazardous waste. The government usually hires private environmental consultants to carry out its cleanup jobs, which include military bases and military production sites.

The United States has some of the toughest environmental laws in the world. Beginning in the 1960s, people began to realize that this country's industries, including its military production industry, were producing vast amounts of pollution and waste that were ruining the environment and threatening human health and safety. Private industry, municipalities, and the government had been producing hazardous and other wastes for many years. A series of tough laws, including CERCLA, have been passed over the last 30 years to force the cleanup of old waste sites and discourage companies from creating new ones. Although the cost of cleaning up our environment is high—billions of dollars have been spent to clean up hazardous waste sites—the cost of not cleaning up is potentially even higher.

REQUIREMENTS
High School
While still in high school, potential hazardous waste management technicians should take math and science, including biology, earth sciences, physics, and chemistry. To hone communication skills, you also should take English, speech, and writing.

Postsecondary Training
In the past, hazardous waste management technicians could find plenty of work with only a high school diploma. Hazardous waste management is becoming an increasingly sophisticated field, however, because of tighter regulations and advances in cleanup technology. More and more, a two-year diploma or degree in hazardous waste management is becoming important for many positions.

There are hundreds of choices for those interested in pursuing postsecondary training in hazardous waste management. Options include community colleges, technical colleges, vocational institutes, and college outreach programs. Students should make sure the school is accredited and talk to the people in the career services office to find out where graduates have gone on to work.

Whether or not a degree is required depends on the task, the company, and the nature of the problem, according to the Air and

Waste Management Association. For some field or monitoring work, two-year degrees may be needed. Some of these jobs involve sophisticated work like chemical analyses or working under protocols.

On the other hand, other technicians are essentially moving waste, like forklift drivers, warehouse workers, or drivers. They will get some particular training or instruction from the company, but generally don't need a degree.

Experts see a trend toward higher educational requirements for environmental technicians overall. This is especially true in hazardous waste management. In this area, technical degrees, even graduate degrees, tend to be valued more than in some other areas, such as solid waste handling.

Certification or Licensing

Hazardous waste management technicians can apply for one or more of the following certifications from the National Environmental Health Association (NEHA): registered environmental health specialist/registered sanitarian, certified environmental health technician, registered hazardous substances professional, registered hazardous substances specialist, registered environmental technician (RET), and the NEHA Radon Proficiency Program. Contact the NEHA for more information on these certifications. Some employers also pay for workshops run in-house by the NEHA and other associations such as the Occupational Safety and Health Administration (OSHA). These workshops educate employees about such topics as emergency response, Superfund regulations, and emerging technologies.

Other Requirements

Hazardous waste management technicians work with toxic and volatile materials. To ensure their own safety and that of others, they must be extremely alert and accurate. They also must be able to follow orders. Some, but not all, positions require technical and scientific aptitude. Hazardous waste management technicians usually work in teams, so they must be able to cooperate and communicate well with others. Good reasoning skills, analytical thinking, and the ability to respond to unexpected conditions are also important.

Technicians must be rule followers and they must be careful listeners. Regulations drive this industry; there are standards and guidelines that must be followed for every part of the hazardous waste management technician's job. If a standard requires the hazardous waste management technician to collect a half-liter sample, he or she must get exactly that. When hazardous waste management technicians do not follow regulations, the price can be high. They can cost their employers or clients a great deal of money in fines, or, worse, they can endanger their lives and the lives of others. Good technicians also must be flexible, able to spot problems, and able to think quickly on their feet.

EXPLORING

If you are interested in exploring careers in hazardous waste management, you should get involved in local chapters of citizen watchdog groups and become familiar with nearby Superfund sites. Ask yourself the following questions: What is being done at those sites? Who is responsible for the cleanup? What effect does the site have on nearby communities? You can also learn more about different types of hazardous waste, and recycling, treatment, and storage tactics by visiting the EPA Web site (http://www.epa.gov/wastes/hazard). Another good resource is the Right to Know Network (http://www.rtknet.org), which provides information about hazardous waste reports, including violations, toxic spills and accidents, civil action cases, legislation updates, and other resources related to environmental issues.

Additionally, understanding the problems of hazardous waste management and the controversy surrounding some of the limitations of Superfund will provide a more detailed picture of careers in this field. Ask your librarian or teacher to refer you to resources or visit the associations listed at the end of this article to gather more information. You might also try to arrange an information interview with a hazardous waste management technician.

EMPLOYERS

Hazardous waste management technicians are employed by chemical companies and other producers of hazardous waste, waste disposal companies and waste disposal consulting engineering firms, environmental consulting firms, government agencies, and other organizations. The largest number of jobs is in the private sector.

Following are some private-sector employers of hazardous waste management technicians.

In-house staffs. Private industry jobs can be found within large companies. Such companies generate waste and are likely to have their own in-house staff of environmentalists. This is especially true as regulations keep getting more and more complex. Medium-sized companies may have smaller departments. Smaller

WORDS TO KNOW

Comprehensive Environmental Response, Compensation, and Liability Act (CERCLA)   1980 law (known as Superfund) that mandated cleanup of private and government-owned hazardous waste sites.

defense waste   Radioactive waste from weapons research and development, decommissioned nuclear-powered ships and submarines, weapons material production, and other military waste; includes low- and high-level radioactive, hazardous, and mixed (radioactive and hazardous) waste.

Level A work   Work involving hazardous substances that pose a high dermal (skin) threat.

sampling   Taking quantities of water, soil, or air from a site. Samples are tested in labs to check for the presence of hazardous substances.

companies may have a professional or two on staff, or hire outside consultants.

Consultants. Consulting companies are another good source of employment opportunities for hazardous waste management technicians. Some consulting companies advise companies on how to handle a hazardous waste problem. Others also design a plan and provide the manpower to carry it out. Some have their own testing and laboratory services.

Following are public-sector employers.

The EPA is just one federal government agency that uses technicians. In fact, says the Environmental Careers Organization, the U.S. Forest Service, the National Park Service, the Bureau of Land Management, and the Fish and Wildlife Service probably employ more technicians and field personnel, while the EPA uses more scientists and other professionals. There also is a trend toward increased work in hazardous waste management at the local level, by states, counties, and municipalities. Jobs there include technicians at municipal water plants and other public facilities.

A growing part of the hazardous waste management field is the handling and disposal of medical wastes. Hospitals, labs, health care facilities, and pharmaceutical companies may have staff personnel to help them take care of their medical wastes or they may hire consultants to do the job. Smaller generators of hazardous wastes include university research facilities and even households. Another source of hazardous waste is inactive mines: Hazardous minerals can leak into nearby surface and groundwater, creating potential health hazards.

STARTING OUT

Most recent graduates and working professionals find jobs through trade association advertisements and on the Internet. Openings with government agencies can be found on the Web page of the Office of Personnel Management (http://www.usajobs.opm.gov). Hazardous waste management technicians can also find job listings on the employment Web site Indeed (http://www.indeed.com).

ADVANCEMENT

Technicians typically don't go on to earn professional degrees. However, there are several other advancement options that may be of interest to technicians. They may, for example, opt to specialize in the disposal of hazardous waste. These people conduct studies on hazardous waste management projects and provide information on treatment and containment of hazardous waste. At the government level, they help to develop hazardous waste rules and regulations.

Technicians can also advance to the position of *incident commander*. An incident commander is the individual who's in charge of and has ultimate responsibility for a hazardous waste site. They supervise workers and meet with state and federal regulatory authorities as necessary.

Obtaining more education and training can help the technician earn more money and take on more responsibility. In some companies, additional education will also earn the technician a higher title.

Some environmental professionals work in community relations or public affairs, helping to inform the public about what a company is doing with its wastes. The government also employs such professionals to help spread information about regulations and cleanup efforts.

EARNINGS

Salaries vary according to position, years of experience, geographic location, and educational background. According to the U.S.

Department of Labor, hazardous materials removal workers had median hourly earnings of $17.94 (or $37,310 annually) in 2008. Wages ranged from less than $11.41 per hour (or $23,740 annually) to more than $30.42 per hour (or $63,260 annually) for full-time work.

Technicians working in industry generally receive benefits that include paid vacation and sick days, as well as health and life insurance. The consulting field may offer bonuses and better opportunities for advancement but generally provides fewer benefits.

WORK ENVIRONMENT

Because of the danger associated with chemical and other types of hazardous waste, technicians must approach potential waste sites with extreme caution. Protective gear is often necessary and can be bulky, interfering with the work. The regulations that control hazardous waste management are complex and increasingly demanding and can slow remediation projects to a frustrating crawl.

Depending on the type of employer, hazardous waste management technicians might do varying degrees of physical labor, work outdoors in all types of weather, and be required to travel considerable distances to investigate and remediate sites. Hazardous waste management technicians work a standard 40-hour week; however, emergency response technicians will stay at critical sites for as long as safety standards permit until the situation is under control. This type of work can account for long hours.

OUTLOOK

The U.S. Department of Labor predicts that employment of hazardous materials management technicians will grow about as fast as the average for all occupations through 2016. Opportunities will be strongest in the private sector as government entities contract out more work to private companies.

FOR MORE INFORMATION

For information on careers and educational programs, contact
Air & Waste Management Association
One Gateway Center, 3rd Floor
420 Fort Duquesne Boulevard
Pittsburgh, PA 15222-1435

Tel: 412-232-3444
Email: info@awma.org
http://www.awma.org

For information on certification for hazardous materials managers, contact

Institute of Hazardous Materials Management
11900 Parklawn Drive, Suite 450
Rockville, MD 20852-2624
Tel: 301-984-8969
Email: ihmminfo@ihmm.org
http://www.ihmm.org

For certification information, contact

National Environmental Health Association
720 South Colorado Boulevard, Suite 1000-N
Denver, CO 80246-1926
Tel: 303-756-9090
Email: staff@neha.org
http://www.neha.org

Land Acquisition Professionals

QUICK FACTS

School Subjects
Business
Earth science

Personal Skills
Communication/ideas
Leadership/management

Work Environment
Indoors and outdoors
One location with some
   travel

Minimum Education Level
Bachelor's degree

Salary Range
$21,860 to $45,000 to
   $102,250+

Certification or Licensing
None available

Outlook
About as fast as the average

OVERVIEW

Land acquisition professionals work with nonprofit organizations to help develop vacant lots and other unused spaces for community benefit, such as for public open spaces. They also help in the efforts of nonprofit land trusts to preserve land and water from urban sprawl, such as housing and shopping center development, subdivision, or other human disruption, by handling the land transaction. Their work involves buying the land outright, acquiring development rights to it, obtaining easements (which means getting permission to use another person's land for a stated purpose), getting landowners to donate the land, or similar actions.

HISTORY

Land acquisitions has evolved as a specialty within nonprofit land trusts, which in turn are a special part of land and water conservation efforts in this country.

Land and water conservation efforts in the United States go back more than 100 years, when the federal government first started setting aside wilderness areas and other open land and water. Since then, hundreds of millions of acres have been preserved in federally owned and managed national parks, wildlife refuges, wild and scenic rivers, and other areas as well as state or locally managed protected lands. Today, acquisition by the federal government is largely complete, but acquisitions by private land trusts continue. The Land Trust Alliance reports that local and regional private, nonprofit land trusts have conserved more than 37 million acres of open space as of 2005—a more than 50 percent increase of the acreage protected as of 2000.

Broadly, land trusts are private nonprofit groups formed to acquire and manage open lands for the public's benefit. The first official land trust in this country was The Trustees of Reservations, formed in Boston in 1891. Concerned that open lands around the city were being rapidly swallowed up by development, this group of private citizens took action: They bought some land themselves and made it available to the public for recreation.

Interest in the United States really took off in the 1960s and 1970s, when awareness and concern about the environment started to grow. In 2005 there were 1,667 private, nonprofit land trusts, ranging from small, one- or two-person trusts to large statewide groups with paid staffs of 30 or more people.

There are also several large national land trust organizations that do land trust work themselves or provide support services to other land trusts and work with government agencies as well. One is The Nature Conservancy (TNC), based in Arlington, Virginia, with state chapters nationwide. Established in 1951, today it employs contract and seasonal workers and emphasizes conservation of "rare or relatively rare" species and natural communities.

San Francisco-based Trust for Public Land (TPL), established in 1972, is another key group. An early TPL success was buying up miles of San Francisco coastline, therefore rescuing it from developers' hands. (The National Park Service now manages these areas.) Today, TPL also provides a wide range of services to other land trusts, from an informational newsletter to help with handling land transactions.

In 1982 the Land Trust Alliance was set up by trusts nationwide that wanted a central organization in Washington, D.C. In addition to providing information services, publications, documents, case studies, and other support to land trusts, it has a lobbyist to give land trusts a presence on Capitol Hill.

The Trustees of Reservations—that first U.S. land trust—still exists today, and is still acquiring land statewide. They currently own and care for more than 100 sites (over 25,000 acres) across Massachusetts. In fact, Massachusetts has the largest number of land trusts of all the states. But land trusts also exist in every other state, doing their part to help keep forests, prairies, coastlines, and other areas intact.

THE JOB

Land acquisition professionals may work independently on one or multiple tasks, or there may be several professionals, with various titles, working to accomplish one task. The job structure and specific responsibilities will depend on the land trust. Larger well-funded land trusts and national land trust organizations are most likely to have acquisitions professionals devoted solely to handling land transactions. In smaller organizations, one person may be responsible for multiple tasks, ranging from negotiating and acquiring land to fund-raising and promotion.

A number of questions need to be addressed before a land trust can save a land or water site. The trust needs to find out who owns the land and if that person or group would be interested in donating the land to the trust; and if the owner is not interested in donating it, would they be willing to sell it, and what would be their sale price. The land trust also needs to find a buyer, which could be a public agency, or a community group that could raise the required funds.

A land trust can check with the local government to see if it is interested in helping to acquire the land. If that does not work, the trust can act on its own, negotiating with the landowner regarding selling or donating the land, pointing out to the owner the many benefits of doing so. The land trust could also solicit assistance from big groups like the Land Trust Alliance, TNC, or TPL. At TPL, for example, project managers are available to help coordinate acquisitions efforts for other land trusts.

Acquisitions may take different forms. One type of acquisition is simply buying the land outright. Another involves acquiring development rights to the land. A third type of acquisition is one in which the landowner maintains ownership, but allows for easements (that is, allowing the land to be used for a specific agreed-upon purpose). Another way to acquire land is to get the landowner to donate the land or leave it to the land trust in his or her will. When selling the land to the land trust, negotiations closely resemble the process involved in buying a house. There is no need to involve the courts. Once the deal has been struck, the land is appraised and the land trust gets the title and deed to the property. The land then becomes the property of the land trust.

For land donations, nonprofits offer certain advantages to land-owners over donating to government or quasi-government groups. Generally, anything donated to a nonprofit is tax deductible. Large landowners may gain certain additional tax benefits by willing the land to a nonprofit when the landowner dies.

In general, most government agencies are not set up to receive donations of land. Landowners also may like the nonprofits' conser-vation emphasis and may not like the idea of donating their land to the government.

Instead of selling, donating, or willing the land, landowners might instead agree to easements that effectively put part of the land off-limits to development, subdivision, or other actions that might threaten preservation. For example, a large paper company gave TNC agricultural and environmental easements on property the paper company owns near Richmond, Virginia, on which stands the oldest working farm in America. As with a land donation, the farmer or landowner who agrees to the easement gets some kind of tax break. In addition to the tax break, the landowner has the pleasure of doing something for the environment.

The reasons vary for how and why a land trust decides upon an area of land or body of water to save. In some cases, it's to ensure that a new residential development has access to green, open park space. In other cases, the issues are much larger, such as protecting an endangered natural community. The Nature Conservancy, for example, emphasizes acquiring areas where there is a threat to a natural community. This may involve endangered species, but TNC also thinks in terms of "rare" and "relatively rare" species, and of the uniqueness of the land—saving areas representing the best of their kind, such as the best oak hardwood forests, for example. Databases help keep track of such efforts.

REQUIREMENTS
High School

Land acquisition professionals bring diverse educational back-grounds to the job. A well-rounded foundation starts in high school, with course work in science, including biology and ecology. Eng-lish and speech classes will help you down the road in negotiating agreements with landowners. Business and math classes are useful for working with contracts and tax documents. Familiarity with a foreign language may be helpful as well.

Postsecondary Training

An undergraduate degree is generally required to work as a land acquisition professional at a land trust. Some prior work experience is also usually required. Good negotiation and deal-making skills are critical to land acquisition professionals. In addition to diverse education backgrounds, people bring diverse work experience to the land trust and preserve field, which serves to enrich the industry even further. They bring a new, fresh perspective to the job that could stem from previous work as a city planner or land-use consultant, or from a background in law or journalism. Land acquisition professionals with real estate experience are particularly useful in this field, as they come armed with knowledge of real estate laws and transactions.

Types of Land Trusts

traditional land trusts   Traditional land trusts hold easements from private landowners who keep their land ownership. Landowners turn their land over to land trusts when they want to do something good for the environment or for historic preservation. Another incentive is that they receive a tax break. Trusts acquire sites to put a stop to excessive grazing, farming, or recreational use of the land; to prevent development of open lands; to clean up ponds, lakes, and restore ecosystems; and to help manage lands with rare or endangered species.

community land trusts (CLTs)   These types of land trusts are actually private, nonprofit corporations created to buy and hold land for the benefit of a community. CLTs are especially focused on meeting the needs of lower-income residents in the community by providing them with secure, affordable access to land and housing. CLTs help communities gain control over local land use and reduce absentee ownership. They promote resident ownership and control of housing, and build a strong base for community action.

Source: Land Trust Alliance, Institute for Community Economics

Other Requirements

Having an understanding of the history of the land and an appreciation for nature and the desire to help preserve it are critical elements of the job. To successfully negotiate land acquisition contracts, strong knowledge of real estate and tax laws is essential. Creative thinkers with clear verbal and written communication skills do best in this type of work.

EXPLORING

You can learn more about this field by reading the book *Conservancy: The Land Trust Movement in America*, by Richard Brewer. You can also learn more about one organization's work to conserve open spaces by visiting the Web site of Project for Public Spaces (http://www.pps.org). And a great way to gain a better appreciation of the importance of land trust work and the magnitude of a land trust's success is through the book *Big Sur and Beyond: The Legacy of the Big Sur Land Trust*, by Clint Eastwood.

STARTING OUT

Volunteering for or doing an internship with a land trust is an excellent way to enter the field. Large statewide organizations are probably the best bets for internships, as are the national organizations. Another great way to get firsthand experience is to start your own land trust. You can learn more about how to do this by visiting the "Start a Land Trust" page on the Land Trust Alliance's Web site (http://www.landtrustalliance.org/conserve/about-land-trusts/start-a-land-trust).

ADVANCEMENT

Advancement will depend on the size of the land trust organization. For example, a project manager with the Trust for Public Land might move up to an administrative position or get more complicated cases. Other options might be to move over to a federal agency that manages federal lands, although these jobs may be scarce, or into the for-profit sector, such as with a consulting firm or a private company that manages large parcels of land, like a timber company. Land acquisition professionals can also expand their knowledge by pursuing advanced degrees, writing books and columns about the land trust field, and teaching at colleges and universities.

EARNINGS

Less than half of land trusts have paid staff. However, executive directors of land trusts may earn salaries that range from $21,860 to $102,250 annually, depending on the size of the trust.

Full-time land trust and preserve managers usually receive fringe benefits such as paid vacation and sick days, health insurance, and 401(k) plans.

WORK ENVIRONMENT

The work environment varies regularly for land acquisition professionals. Some days (and even weeks) may be spent indoors in the office handling phone calls and emails, as well as visiting landowners' offices to negotiate acquisition contracts. Other days may be spent out in the field, and this can be quite literally in a field, checking land or water parcels. Land acquisition professionals will travel to wherever the site is, whether close by or on the other side of the country. Work hours and benefits will vary depending on the size of the land trust and its resources.

OUTLOOK

Public awareness and concern about protecting the environment and preserving open spaces for future generations is ensuring work for land trust professionals in the years to come. According to the Land Trust Alliance, new land trusts are developing regularly. There are some old ones that have celebrated their 100th anniversary, but many are much younger. Just 53 land trusts operated in 26 states in 1950. That number has increased 30 times over since then: Today, more than 1,700 land trusts operate across the United States, serving every state in the nation. The Northeast holds the record for the highest number of land trusts (581) in the country, according to a recent LTA National Land Trust Census.

FOR MORE INFORMATION

Learn more about community land trusts by visiting ICE's Web site.

Institute for Community Economics (ICE)
1101 30th Street, NW, Suite 400
Washington, DC 20007-3771
Tel: 202-333-8931
http://www.iceclt.org

Learn more about programs and events in your region, and stay up to date on land conservation policies and initiatives by visiting LTA's Web site.

Land Trust Alliance (LTA)
1660 L Street, NW, Suite 1100
Washington, DC 20036-5635
Tel: 202-638-4725
Email: info@lta.org
http://www.landtrustalliance.org

Find information about internships with TNC state chapters or at the TNC headquarters by visiting

The Nature Conservancy (TNC)
4245 North Fairfax Drive, Suite 100
Arlington, VA 22203-1606
Tel: 703-841-5300
http://nature.org

This group helps to protect and restore national parks, marine sanctuaries, cultural landmarks, and community green spaces throughout the country. Find out about internships and jobs by visiting

Student Conservation Association
PO Box 550
689 River Road
Charlestown, NH 03603-0550
Tel: 603-543-1700
http://www.thesca.org

For information on land conservation careers, contact

The Trust for Public Land
116 New Montgomery Street, 4th Floor
San Francisco, CA 94105-3638
Tel: 415-495-4014
Email: info@tpl.org
http://www.tpl.org

Land Trust or Preserve Managers

School Subjects
Biology
Earth science

Personal Skills
Communication/ideas
Leadership/management

Work Environment
Primarily outdoors
One location with some
travel

Minimum Education Level
Bachelor's degree

Salary Range
$33,102 to $65,573 to
$120,000+

Certification or Licensing
None available

Outlook
About as fast as the average

OVERVIEW

Land trust or preserve managers work for private or federal organizations that are dedicated to preserving areas of land or bodies of water from development; subdivision; pollution; and overuse by recreational activities, agricultural operations, or other human actions. Managers' responsibilities are diverse, ranging from monitoring the site and inventorying species to managing natural resources. They may also work on specialized conservation and preservation projects, such as re-creating lost or damaged ecosystems, restoring native plants and animals, or conducting controlled burnings.

HISTORY

Government and private citizens' or community groups have driven the land and water conservation efforts in the United States for more than 100 years. In the late 1800s awareness about the quickly diminishing wilderness areas in the West inspired the U.S. government to establish the first national parks and preserves. Yellowstone

National Park was the first national park in the world, established in 1872. The government also set aside four Civil War battlefields as national battlefield parks.

Theodore Roosevelt, the 26th president of the United States, played a pivotal role in the early days of conservation. Roosevelt purchased and maintained a ranch in the Dakota Badlands in the late 1800s. The experience helped him heal from personal tragedies and inspired him to write many books and articles about his time there. He fell in love with the West's vast open spaces and wildlife, and gained a deeper appreciation for nature. When Roosevelt became president in 1901, he used the position to help preserve the West. His administration pushed conservation as part of an overall strategy for the responsible use of natural resources, including forests, pastures, fish, game, soil, and minerals. As a result, public awareness of and support for conservation increased, and important early conservation legislation was enacted. A particular focus of Roosevelt's administration was the preservation of forests, wildlife, parklands, wilderness areas, and watershed areas, and it carried out such work as the first inventory of natural resources in this country.

Individual citizens are also part of the conservation movement's backbone. They have helped save numerous acres of land and water by forming private nonprofit land trusts and establishing national nonprofit land trust organizations.

One example of early citizens' conservation action took place in 1891 in Boston. At that time, the city was booming thanks to a thriving shipbuilding industry plus other commercial and industrial pursuits. Boston also had seen an explosion in its immigrant population, particularly Irish immigrants. In addition, the captains of industry and their families invested heavily in the arts, adding to Boston's reputation as the "Athens of America."

While many saw this as a rich, affluent time in Boston, some residents were deeply concerned about the fast urban development that was taking place. The city was spreading out fast and taking over more and more open space—the wild areas that remained were going to disappear, and there would be no respite from city living. People would have no access to open, wild land.

To address this, Boston citizens created the Trustees of Reservations. They bought some of the undeveloped land themselves, and opened the areas to the public for recreational use. The Trustees of Reservations was the first official land trust in the country, and it paved the way for a whole movement of private land trusts.

Individuals as well as large groups have started land trusts; they have worked to protect just a few acres of land up to hundreds of acres, depending on the part of the country and the trust's resources. Sometimes trusts acquire the land or easements on it; but sometimes, and increasingly in recent years, they also take steps to environmentally manage it.

Land trusts saw very strong growth in the mid- to late-1980s, experienced a slight slowdown during the recession in the 1990s, and are now regaining strength due to a resurgence of interest in land and wildlife conservation and preservation. In 2005 there were 1,667 private nonprofit land trusts, up nearly four times the number of trusts (450) that existed in 1982. And according to the Land Trust Alliance, a Washington, D.C.-based organization of 1.5 million land trust supporters and members, the total number of acres protected by local, state, and national land trusts increased by more than 50 percent to 37 million between 2000 and 2005.

Land trusts sometimes work in cooperation with U.S. federal agencies for managing lands. The Nature Conservancy (TNC), for example, a very large national land trust organization specializing in rare wildlife and habitats assists agencies such as the Environmental Protection Agency, the Department of Agriculture, the U.S. Agency for International Development, the Department of the Interior, the National Park Service, and the Department of Defense with the management of land and biodiversity conservation. The conservancy also works with state and local governments, nonprofit organizations, corporations, and private individuals.

Consulting firms specializing in land trust or preserve management can also help with special areas like ecosystem restoration or forestry management. Private corporations, such as utility companies or timber companies, that own and manage large parcels of land

Teddy Roosevelt's Conservation Efforts

All of this landmark conservation legislation was passed during the administration of President Theodore Roosevelt (1901–1909):
- 1902: Reclamation Act
- 1903: Public Lands Commission
- 1905: First National Forest Congress
- 1907: Waterways Commission
- 1908: U.S. Reclamation Service

may also have conservation and preservation efforts in areas such as forest wetlands.

THE JOB

Land trust or preserve managers work for land trusts that acquire land by buying it, getting the landowner to donate it, arranging for easements on it (meaning permission to use the land while the landowner retains ownership), or purchasing the development rights to it. In smaller organizations the land trust employee will have multiple responsibilities. In larger land trusts a staff will handle various tasks, and the sole focus of one of the jobs may be the negotiation and purchase of the land.

What is involved with managing a land trust or preserve? That depends on the specific land or water involved and its needs, who is doing the managing, how much funding and staffing is available, and other factors.

Staffing of land trusts can be minimal, particularly in the early years of the trust. As with any start-up business, in the beginning one person might do everything from handling correspondence to walking the land. If the land trust grows larger, it may add more people who can then focus on specific tasks, including managing the land, handling fund-raising, planning events, reaching out to members, and more. Some land trusts, particularly large statewide land trusts, are large enough to have a full-time, paid staff of up to 30 people.

Federally managed lands can also have varying levels of staffing and funding that determine what specific work can be done. In general, however, federal agencies have greater resources than private land trusts, and the federal government employs about 75 percent of all people working in land and water conservation. For example, all national parks have natural resource management departments that carry out tasks ranging from ensuring environmental compliance to specialized conservation and preservation work.

Specific work varies in different parts of the country, from Eastern forests to the Everglades to coastal areas, and ranges from simply monitoring the land to doing specialized work like re-creating destroyed ecosystems. The following paragraphs detail some of the work carried out by land trust or preserve managers.

Habitat protection. Protecting wildlife habitats, particularly those of rare or endangered species, is intrinsic to the job. The U.S. Fish and Wildlife Service cites that at least 1,317 plants and animals in the United States alone are currently endangered or threatened.

Planning for better use of land and water. If the land is a recreational area, for example, managers might plan how to prevent overuse.

Species inventory. Cataloging plant and animal species helps establish the baseline needed to create short- and long-term plans for the land.

Restoration or re-creation of damaged or destroyed ecosystems. Getting an area back to how it used to be may involve cleaning up pollution, bringing back native species, and getting rid of nonnative species. Landscape architects, biologists, botanists, ecologists, and others may help do such work. Restoration of wetlands, for example, may involve wetlands ecologists, fish and wildlife scientists, and botanists.

Prescribed burnings. It may sound counterproductive, but controlled burnings can actually help in the management of prairies, forests, or rangelands. After the fire, specialists may go in and inventory species. Pitch pine communities in New York and New Jersey, and long-leaf pine forests in Virginia, Texas, and other parts of the South, are just some areas handled in this way.

Rangeland management. To keep plant life reigned in, controlled grazing by bison or cattle is another form of rangeland management.

REQUIREMENTS
High School
While in high school, take classes in biology, chemistry, physics, botany, and ecology. Land trust or preserve managers need strong communication skills for their work in negotiating contracts and managing staff. English and writing classes will help in this arena, as will course work in business and computer software programs. Foreign language classes can also be useful.

Postsecondary Training
A bachelor's degree in a natural science, such as zoology, biology, or botany, can provide a solid foundation for future land trust or preserve work. Employers have also been increasingly interested in seeing candidates who have degrees in conservation biology, which focuses on the conservation of specific plant and animal communities. Schools such as the University of Wisconsin—Madison (http://www.wisc.edu) and the School of Forestry and

(continues on page 138)

 **INTERVIEW**

Robert Linck is the director of conservation funding for the Vermont Land Trust (VLT) in Montpelier, Vermont.

Q. What do you do in your job?
A. I work with regional directors to pick projects that need extra funding. We'll choose two to four, and then talk to people to raise the money. We look at foundation sources and all the ways it can take to raise money. I work with field team members and meet with supporters, gauge their interest, and solicit gifts for specific projects as well as for general support. Fundraising and foundation work is a work in progress. We have tapped less private funding because we've been fortunate with our funding sources. I'll be helping to beef up the cultivation of foundations. With the new [Obama] administration, we will see more resources go to conservation, so we'll be working on this.

Q. What did you do in your previous position?
A. I co-directed the land conservation activities of the Vermont Land Trust's Champlain Valley Region and helped manage the staff, operations, and budget for a six-person office. I assessed the conservation values of land according to land trust criteria; negotiated or managed negotiations with landowners in conservation transactions; raised funds for conservation transactions from foundations, state and federal sources, communities, and individual donors; conducted outreach to landowners, communities, other nonprofit organizations, and the general public; represented the Vermont Land Trust before town boards, state agencies, the legislature, and the media; worked with other staff on organizational policy and systems issues; and assisted headquarters staff with annual and spring fund-raising appeals and membership events.

Q. What do you like most about your work?
A. I like meeting people, learning what interests them in conservation, and what brought them into supporting the organization. We do a lot of work with farmers, with the farm economy— helping to determine the best soils to be farmed, making sure the land is used well. We work with communities on things

that are important to them, and on things that are important to society. We touch on that all the time. Getting transactions completed is satisfying.

Q. What is your work environment like?

A. I work in a very positive and relatively fast-paced environment with dedicated coworkers, in a very well-run nonprofit organization. Our office is in a small town in a rural Vermont setting.

Q. What has surprised you most about this work?

A. The most surprising thing about the work is how deeply satisfying it is. I've been interested in this since the early 1970s, and at it as a career for 30 years. The results are so tangible: You conserve land. Our work is permanent. We can see the benefits. The public can see the benefits. Another surprising thing, though not a positive one, is that you don't get outside as much as you might think. You interact with legal folks, sit in lots of meetings, and work on the computer. You may visit the property two or three times, but that can be it for outside work.

Q. What expectations did you have when you first entered this field?

A. I suppose I had fairly clear expectations when I entered land conservation work, in part because one of my college professors was associated with a local land trust. My first job involved a broad range of responsibilities, including land conservation, so I immediately immersed myself in the kind of work that I have come back to years later. Perhaps one misconception was laid to rest early on—most land trust employees do not spend vast amounts of their time outdoors. The other thing to note is that, perhaps like most jobs, much of what you learn happens on the job.

Q. What other types of positions have you held?

A. I was regional (Vermont/New Hampshire) director for a four-state watershed organization—the Connecticut River

(continues)

(continued)

Watershed Council; conservation director for the Adirondack Mountain Club; recycling coordinator for Warren County, N.Y.; an adjunct professor of environmental studies at Adirondack Community College; an extension specialist for the Hudson River Estuary, New York Sea Grant/Cornell University; associate director for the Upper Valley Land Trust, Hanover, New Hampshire; and executive director of the Southeast Arizona Land Trust.

Q. What advice would you give to someone who is interested in pursuing a career in land trust or preserve management?

A. Fully understand the skill set required for the position you desire, take advantage of training opportunities, seek college- and/or graduate-level education in existing or emerging programs that emphasize land conservation or a key skill associated with land conservation, and pursue opportunities to volunteer or intern at a land trust.

Many land trust jobs involve the type of work described above. Many other positions are focused on management and administration, geographic information systems (GIS) and mapping, fund-raising and community relations, or legal/paralegal work. For land trusts that own land and emphasize ownership and management of land or preserves, some positions will involve much more work outdoors, "in the field." Land trusts (including the Vermont Land Trust) that emphasize the stewardship of conservation easements have positions oriented toward landowner relations, "baseline documentation" of properties that have been conserved (GIS and mapping, field work with maps, GPS operation), field monitoring of private or public conserved land, interpretation of legal documents, and managing a legal process when conservation-easement violations occur.

(continued from page 135)

Environmental Studies (http://environment.yale.edu) at Yale University offer these programs of study.

Robert Linck, director of conservation funding at the Vermont Land Trust in Montpelier, Vermont, says his educational background and internship experiences have helped him in his career. He has a bachelor's of science in environmental studies and biology, and a master's in water resources management and, between those two degrees, he worked for five years for a nonprofit watershed organization.

Other Requirements

Dedicated, hard-working, organized individuals with good communication skills do well in this field. Another requirement is the ability to juggle projects and interact with a wide variety of people.

Land trusts tend to be entrepreneurial. Strong knowledge of business administration, finance, and law, as well as land conservation techniques, will be useful in the job, especially if the tasks involve running the financial end of the trust, raising funds, negotiating deals, and handling tax matters.

EXPLORING

Read books about land and water conservation, such as *Conservancy: The Land Trust Movement in America*, by Richard Brewer, and *Nature's Keepers: The Remarkable Story of How the Nature Conservancy Became the Largest Environmental Group in the World*, by Bill Birchard. You can also learn more about the field by visiting the Web sites of groups such as the Nature Conservancy and the Land Trust Alliance, as well as many others. Read up on their current projects and see if there are any opportunities to volunteer.

EMPLOYERS

The federal government, in its various agencies and branches, is the largest employer of land trust professionals. State and local government agencies also employ some land trust professionals in a variety of positions. Outside of government, potential employers include nonprofit organizations and private land trusts. Other employers of land trust specialists include large banks and other similar institutions.

STARTING OUT

Land trust or preserve management is a popular field, and people start their careers in a variety of ways, such as through a summer or seasonal job, an internship, volunteer work, or a contract project.

Even people graduating with a master's degree may only be able to land contract work at first, which is work done on a per-project or freelance basis (you sign on for one specific project and move on when it is complete). Contract workers usually are specialists, such as ecologists or botanists. The need for them is high in the summer months when biological inventorying work is plentiful.

Robert Linck suggests looking for job listings through the Web sites of the Land Trust Alliance, the Nature Conservancy, and the Trust for Public Land. Volunteer and internship opportunities are also available at many environmental organizations. Getting a foot in the door is the first step, which can provide valuable firsthand experience and may even lead to a paid position.

ADVANCEMENT

Land trust professionals advance in different ways. The traditional promotion path might begin with an internship, then progress to positions of increasing power and responsibility. Another advancement path involves expansion of duties within a specialty field. For example, someone who starts out as a land protection specialist in North Carolina may not have any desire to move out of that work; therefore, his or her job may be expanded laterally—broadening into consulting work in the specialty in other parts of the state, or even nationwide. A third advancement path may be in the form of a "demotion," in which the manager relinquishes administrative duties and goes back to land protection and conservation fieldwork. Land protection specialists may also branch out into writing and teaching.

EARNINGS

According to a 2007 salary survey by the Land Trust Alliance, individuals working in the areas of land easement and stewardship and land protection earned salaries ranging from $33,102 to $56,065, depending on level of experience. The survey also reported that executive directors of land trusts had annual incomes ranging from $65,573 to $80,000 or higher. Salaries also vary by region. For example, according to the survey, executive directors in the Midwest averaged about $66,792 per year, while executive directors in the Pacific region reported annual incomes of $84,170. Also, the higher the land trust's operating budget, the higher the salaries; for example, the LTA survey reported that land trusts with operating budgets of $2 million or more paid executive directors median annual salaries of $120,000. Graduates with a bachelor's degree in conservation and renewable natural resources received an average starting salary offer of $34,678 in July 2007, according to the National Association of Colleges and Employers. Federal government agency jobs pay more than state or local government jobs. Nonprofit groups' salaries can be competitive but tend to be at the lower end of the pay range.

WORK ENVIRONMENT

The work may be indoors, outdoors, or a combination of both, depending on the job. Fieldwork will involve working outdoors in a natural area, on land and water, taking notes and inventorying plant and animal species. The work may require a certain amount of walking and hiking, or even rowing a boat. Administrators, communicators, lawyers, and others in more advanced positions usually work in offices, especially if they are working for larger organizations. People in this field are extremely dedicated to their jobs and enjoy their work.

OUTLOOK

Robert Linck says the future of this field is very promising. "Over 1,600 land trusts operate around the United States today, and the numbers are still growing. Though some of them are very small and may involve only volunteers, many more are already large organizations or are growing, so land conservation continues to have a strong future. We won't be doing land conservation forever. There will be a saturation point in different areas. There will come a point when people will say, 'When are we going to stop doing this here?' There will be fewer projects done, but land trusts are perpetual. You are fund-raising to draw money for endorsements. You may not own the land, but you maintain relationships with the landowners. And you continue to visit the land. We're endowed to do this. We'll be doing this forever, for however long that is. So it's a secure job, in that sense, for people who are doing this type of work."

The best employment opportunities can be found with private land trusts and national land trust organizations. Land trusts are the fastest-growing arm of the conservation movement today, with 1,667 operating in the United States in 2005, according to the Land Trust Alliance (LTA), each protecting more land every year. In an LTA national land trust census, statistics showed that local and regional land trusts protected nearly 37 million acres as of 2005, which was more than double the amount of acreage protected in 2000.

FOR MORE INFORMATION

Learn more about land trusts and find offices, resources, and programs in your region by visiting

Land Trust Alliance
1600 L Street, NW, Suite 1100
Washington, DC 20036-5635
Tel: 202-638-4725
Email: info@lta.org
http://www.landtrustalliance.org

This conservation organization offers fellowships for graduate work in conservation, places people in paid internships, and more.

National Wildlife Federation
11100 Wildlife Center Drive
Reston, VA 20190-5362
Tel: 800-822-9919
http://www.nwf.org

Find information about internships with TNC state chapters or at the TNC headquarters by visiting

The Nature Conservancy (TNC)
4245 North Fairfax Drive, Suite 100
Arlington, VA 22203-1606
Tel: 703-841-5300
http://www.nature.org

Learn more about volunteer positions in natural resource management by visiting

Student Conservation Association
PO Box 550
689 River Road
Charlestown, NH 03603-0550
Tel: 603-543-1700
http://www.thesca.org

For information on land conservation careers, contact

The Trust for Public Land
116 New Montgomery Street, 4th Floor

San Francisco, CA 94105-3638
Tel: 415-495-4014
Email: info@tpl.org
http://www.tpl.org

Park Rangers

OVERVIEW

Park rangers enforce laws and regulations in national, state, and county parks. They help care for and maintain parks as well as inform, guide, and ensure the safety of park visitors.

HISTORY

Congress established The National Park System in the United States in 1872 when Yellowstone National Park was created. The National Park Service (NPS), a bureau of the U.S. Department of the Interior, was created in 1916 to preserve, protect, and manage the national, cultural, historical, and recreational areas of the National Park System. At that time, the park system contained less than 1 million acres. Today, the country's national parks cover about 84 million acres of mountains, plains, deserts, swamps, historic sites, lakeshores, forests, rivers, battlefields, memorials, archaeological properties, and recreation areas.

All NPS areas are given one of the following designations: National Park, National Historical Park, National Battlefield, National Battlefield Site, National Cemetery, National Military Site, National Memorial, National Historic Site, National Monument, National

Preserve, National Seashore, National Parkway, National Lakeshore, National River, National Trail, National Wild and Scenic River, National Recreation Area, or just Park. (The White House in Washington, D.C., for example, which is administered by the NPS, is officially a Park.)

To protect the fragile, irreplaceable resources located in these areas, and to protect the millions of visitors who climb, ski, hike, boat, fish, and otherwise explore them, the National Park Service employs park rangers. State and county parks employ rangers to perform similar tasks.

THE JOB

Park rangers have a wide variety of duties that range from conservation efforts to bookkeeping. Their first responsibility is, however, safety. Rangers who work in parks with treacherous terrain, dangerous wildlife, or severe weather must make sure hikers, campers, and backpackers follow outdoor safety codes. They often require visitors to register at park offices so that rangers will know when someone does not return from a hike or climb and may be hurt. Rangers often participate in search-and-rescue missions for visitors who are lost or injured. In mountainous or forested regions, they may use helicopters or horses for searches.

Rangers also protect parks from inappropriate use and other threats from humans. They register vehicles and collect parking and registration fees, which are used to help maintain roads and facilities. They enforce the laws, regulations, and policies of the parks, patrolling to prevent vandalism, theft, and harm to wildlife. Rangers may arrest and evict people who violate these laws. Some of their efforts to conserve and protect park resources include keeping jeeps and other motorized vehicles off sand dunes and other fragile lands. They make sure visitors do not litter, pollute water, chop down trees for firewood, or start unsafe campfires that could lead to catastrophic forest fires. When forest fires do start, rangers often help with the dangerous and arduous task of putting them out.

Park rangers carry out various tasks associated with the management of the natural resources within the National Park System. An important aspect of this responsibility is the care and management of both native and exotic animal species found within the boundaries of the parks. Duties may include conducting basic research and disseminating information about the reintroduction of native animal populations and the protection of the natural habitat that supports the animals.

Rangers also help with conservation, research, and ecology efforts that are not connected to visitors' use of the park. They may study wildlife behavior patterns, for example, by tagging and following certain animals. In this way they can chart the animals' migration patterns, assess the animals' impact on the park's ecosystem, and determine whether the park should take measures to control or encourage certain wildlife populations.

Some rangers study plant life and may work with conservationists to reintroduce native or endangered species. They measure the quality of water and air in the park to monitor and mitigate the effects of pollution and other threats from sources outside park boundaries.

In addition, park rangers help visitors enjoy and experience parks. In historical and other cultural parks, such as the Alamo in San Antonio, Texas, Independence Hall in Philadelphia, and the Lincoln Home in Springfield, Illinois, rangers give lectures and provide guided tours explaining the history and significance of the site. In natural parks, they may lecture on conservation topics, provide information about plants and animals in the park, and take visitors on interpretive walks, pointing out the area's flora, fauna, and geological characteristics. At a Civil War battlefield park, such as Gettysburg National Military Park in Pennsylvania or Vicksburg National Military Park in Mississippi, they explain to visitors what happened at that site during the Civil War and its implications for our country.

Park rangers are also indispensable to the management and administration of parks. They issue permits to visitors and vehicles and help plan the recreational activities in parks. They help in the planning and managing of park budgets. They keep records and compile statistics concerning weather conditions, resource conservation activities, and the number of park visitors.

Many rangers supervise other workers in the parks who build and maintain park facilities, work part time or seasonally, or operate concession facilities. Rangers often have their own park maintenance responsibilities, such as trail building, landscaping, and caring for visitor centers. They may also operate campsites, which might entail assigning sites to campers, replenishing firewood, and performing safety inspections.

In some parks rangers are specialists in certain areas of park protection, safety, or management. For example, in areas with heavy snowfall and a high incidence of avalanches, experts in avalanche control and snow safety are designated snow rangers. They monitor snow conditions and patrol park areas to make sure visitors are not lost in snowslides.

REQUIREMENTS
High School

To prepare for the necessary college course load, you should take courses in earth science, biology, mathematics, English, and speech. Any classes or activities that deal with plant and animal life, the weather, geography, and interacting with others will be helpful.

Park rangers must enforce laws as well as inform and guide park visitors. *Lawrence Migdale/Photo Researchers, Inc.*

Postsecondary Training

Employment as a federal or state park ranger requires either a college degree or a specific amount of education and experience. Approximately 200 colleges and universities offer bachelor's degree programs in park management and park recreation. To meet employment requirements, students in other relevant college programs must accumulate at least 24 semester hours of academic credit in park recreation and management, history, behavioral sciences, forestry, botany, geology, or other applicable subject areas.

Without a degree, you will need three years of experience in parks or conservation and you must show an understanding of what is required in park work. In addition, you must demonstrate good communication skills. A combination of education and experience can also fulfill job requirements, with one academic year of study equaling nine months of experience. Also, the orientation and training a ranger receives on the job may be supplemented with formal training courses.

To succeed as a ranger, you will need skills in protecting forests, parks, and wildlife and in interpreting natural or historical resources. Law enforcement and management skills are also important. If you wish to move into management positions, you may need a graduate degree. Approximately 50 universities offer master's degrees in park recreation and management, and 16 have doctoral programs.

Certification or Licensing

Certification is not required but can broaden a park ranger's education. Employers also look favorably upon certification because it shows commitment to the career and mastery of certain advanced aspects of the work. The National Recreation and Park Association (NRPA) provides certification to park and recreation professionals who pass an exam and have a bachelor's degree in recreation, park resources, or leisure services from an NRPA-accredited program, or a BA and five years of relevant work experience.

Other Requirements

In order to be a good park ranger, you should believe in the importance of the country's park resources and the mission of the park system. If you enjoy working outdoors, independently and with others, you may enjoy park ranger work. Rangers need self-confidence, patience, and the ability to stay levelheaded during emergencies. To participate in rescues, you need courage, physical stamina, and endurance, and to deal with visitors you must have tact, sincerity, a personable nature, and a sense of humor. A sense of camaraderie among fellow rangers can make the job more fun.

EXPLORING

The best way to explore park ranger work is to get a part-time or seasonal job in a national, state, or county park. This type of work usually entails maintenance and other unskilled tasks, but it also provides opportunities to observe park rangers and talk with them about their day-to-day tasks. You might also try working as a volunteer. Many park research activities, study projects, and rehabilitation efforts are conducted by volunteer groups affiliated with universities or conservation organizations. These activities can provide insight into the work done by park rangers.

EMPLOYERS

Park rangers in the National Park Service are employed by the U.S. Department of the Interior. There are approximately 20,000 permanent, temporary, and seasonal employees in the National Park Service. Rangers may also be employed by other federal agencies or by state and county agencies in charge of their respective parks.

STARTING OUT

Many workers enter national park ranger jobs after working part time or seasonally at different parks. These workers often work at information desks or in fire control or law enforcement positions. Some help maintain trails, collect trash, or perform forestry activities. If you are interested in applying for a park ranger job with the federal government, contact your local Federal Job Information Center or the Federal Office of Personnel Management in Washington, D.C., for application information. To find jobs in state parks, you should write to the appropriate state departments for information.

ADVANCEMENT

Nearly all rangers start in entry-level positions, which means that nearly all higher-level openings are filled via the promotion of current workers. Entry-level rangers may move into such positions as *district ranger* or *park manager*, or they may become specialists in resource management or park planning. Rangers who show management skills and become park managers may move into administrative positions in the district, regional, or national headquarters.

The orientation and training a ranger receives on the job may be supplemented with formal training courses. Training for job skills unique to the National Park Service is available at the Horace M. Albright Training Center at Grand Canyon National Park in Arizona and the Stephen T. Mather Training Center at Harpers Ferry, West Virginia. In addition, training is available at the Training Center in New Brunswick, Georgia.

EARNINGS

Rangers in the National Park Service are usually hired at the GS-5 grade level, which in 2009 translated to earnings of between $30,772 and $40,005 annually. The average ranger is generally at about the second step of the GS-7 level, which translates to a salary of $39,388. The most experienced rangers can earn $49,553, the highest salary step in the GS-7 level.

To move beyond this level, most rangers must become supervisors, subdistrict rangers, district rangers, or division chiefs. At these higher levels, workers can earn more than $87,000 per year. These positions are difficult to obtain, however, because the turnover rate for positions above the GS-7 level is exceptionally low.

In addition to annual salaries, park rangers may receive other benefits, including paid vacations, sick leave, paid holidays, health and life insurance, pension plans, and housing for rangers who work in remote areas.

WORK ENVIRONMENT

Rangers work in parks all over the country, from the Okefenokee Swamp in Florida to the Rocky Mountains of Colorado. They work in the mountains and forests of Hawaii, Alaska, and California and in urban and suburban parks throughout the United States.

National park rangers are hired to work 40 hours per week, but their actual working hours can be long and irregular, with a great deal of overtime. They may receive extra pay or time off for working overtime. Some rangers are on call 24 hours a day for emergencies. Rangers work longer hours during peak tourist seasons. Although many rangers work in offices, many also work outside in all kinds of climates and weather, and most work in a combination of the two settings. Workers may be called upon to risk their own health to

National Park Stats

- In 2006 the National Park System comprised 391 areas covering more than 84 million acres in all U.S. states (except Delaware), the District of Columbia, American Samoa, Guam, Puerto Rico, and the Virgin Islands.
- In 2006 there were more than 272 million visitors to national parks and sites.
- The largest national park is Wrangell-St. Elias National Park and Preserve in south-central Alaska, boasting 13.2 million acres.
- At 0.2 acres, Thaddeus Kosciuszko National Memorial in Philadelphia, Pennsylvania, is the smallest national park.

Source: National Park Service

rescue injured visitors in cold, snow, rain, and darkness. Rangers in Alaska must adapt to long daylight hours in the summer and short daylight hours in the winter. Working outdoors in beautiful surroundings, however, can be wonderfully stimulating and rewarding for the right kind of worker.

OUTLOOK

The U.S. Department of Labor predicts that employment of recreation workers in general will grow about as fast as the average for all occupations through 2016. Competition is and will continue to be keen for park ranger jobs, however, as the work is very interesting and attracts far more applicants than openings. Applicants will have an advantage in the job hunt if they attain the greatest number and widest variety of applicable skills possible. They may wish to study subjects they can use in other fields: forestry, land management, conservation, wildlife management, history, and natural sciences, among others.

In economic downturns more people turn to parks and outdoor recreation as affordable leisure-time activities. Ranger jobs will continue to be important in helping people learn the history of the parks and conservation efforts. Job seekers may also wish to apply for outdoor work with agencies other than the National Park

Top 10 Most Visited National Parks (2008)

1. Great Smoky Mountains (Tennessee,
   North Carolina)   9,044,010
2. Grand Canyon (Arizona)   4,425,314
3. Yosemite (California)   3,431,514
4. Olympic (Washington)   3,081,451
5. Yellowstone (Wyoming, Montana, Idaho)   3,066,580
6. Cuyahoga Valley (Ohio)   2,828,233
7. Rocky Mountain (Colorado)   2,757,390
8. Zion (Utah)   2,690,154
9. Grand Teton (Wyoming)   2,485,987
10. Acadia (Maine)   2,075,857

Source: National Parks Conservation Association

Service, including other federal land and resource management agencies and similar state and local agencies; such agencies usually have more openings.

FOR MORE INFORMATION

For information about state parks and employment opportunities, contact

National Association of State Park Directors
8829 Woodyhill Road
Raleigh, NC 27613-1134
Tel: 919-676-8365
Email: NASPD@me.com
http://www.naspd.org

For general career information, contact the following organizations:

National Parks Conservation Association
1300 19th Street, NW, Suite 300
Washington, DC 20036-1628
Tel: 800-628-7275
Email: npca@npca.org
http://www.npca.org/

National Recreation and Park Association
22377 Belmont Ridge Road
Ashburn, VA 20148-4150
Tel: 800-626-6772
Email: info@nrpa.org
http://www.nrpa.org

Find park ranger job listings, salary information, and other resources at
Park Ranger Jobs
http://www.rangercareers.com

For information on volunteer opportunities, contact
Student Conservation Association
689 River Road
PO Box 550
Charlestown, NH 03603-0550
Tel: 603-543-1700
http://www.thesca.org

For information on federal employment, contact
USAJOBS
Office of Personnel Management
http://www.usajobs.opm.gov

For specific information about careers and job openings with the national parks, contact
U.S. Department of the Interior
National Park Service
1849 C Street, NW
Washington, DC 20240-0001
Tel: 202-208-6843
http://www.nps.gov

Further Reading

Bhatia, S. C. *Solid and Hazardous Waste Management.* New Delhi, India: Atlantic Publishers & Distributors, 2007.

Birchard, Richard. *Nature's Keepers: The Remarkable Story of How the Nature Conservancy Became the Largest Environmental Group in the World.* San Francisco: Jossey-Bass, 2005.

Blackman Jr., William C. *Basic Hazardous Waste Management.* 3d ed. New York: CRC Press, 2001.

Brinkley, Douglas. *The Wilderness Warrior: Theodore Roosevelt and the Crusade for America.* New York: Harper, 2009.

Callies, Bill. *They Used to Call Us Game Wardens.* Hibbing, Minn.: Callies/Hanson Publishing, 2006.

Carson, Rachel. *Silent Spring* (40th anniversary edition). New York: Mariner Books, 2001.

Chapin, Tom. *Poachers Caught!: Adventures of a Northwoods Game Warden.* Cambridge, Minn.: Adventure Publications, 2007.

Chasek, Pamela S. et al. *Global Environmental Politics.* 4th ed. Boulder, Colo.: Westview Press, 2006.

Cohen, Steven et al. *The Effective Public Manager: Achieving Success in a Changing Government.* San Francisco: Jossey-Bass, 2008.

Collin, Robin W. *The Environmental Protection Agency: Cleaning Up America's Act (Understanding of Government).* Santa Barbara, Calif.: Greenwood Press, 2005.

Deal, Kevin H. *Wildlife & Natural Resource Management.* 2d ed. Florence, Ky.: Delmar Cengage Learning, 2002.

Duncan, Dayton and Ken Burns. *The National Parks: America's Best Idea.* New York: Knopf, 2009.

Fairfax, Sally K. et al. *Buying Nature: The Limits of Land Acquisition as a Conservation Strategy, 1780–2004.* Cambridge, Mass.: The MIT Press, 2005.

Farabee, Charles R. Butch. *National Park Ranger: An American Icon.* Lanham, Md.: Roberts Rinehart Publishers, 2003.

Festa-Bianchet, Marco and Marco Apollinio, eds. *Animal Behavior and Wildlife Conservation.* Washington, D.C.: Island Press, 2003.

Frumkin, Howard. *Environmental Health: From Global to Local.* San Francisco: Jossey-Bass, 2005.

Ginn, William. *Investing in Nature: Case Studies of Land Conservation in Collaboration with Business.* Washington, D.C.: Island Press, 2005.

Greenland, Paul R. and Annamarie L. Sheldon. *Career Opportunities in Conservation and the Environment.* New York: Checkmark Books, 2007.

Groom, Martha J. et al. *Principles of Conservation Biology.* 3d ed. Sunderland, Mass.: Sinauer Associates, 2005.

Hagan, Pat. *Seasonal Disorder: Ranger Tales from Glacier National Park.* Boulder, Colo.: Johnson Books, 2006.

Hethcox, Jim. *Adventures in Green & Gray: True Stories of a Game Warden.* LaGrange, Ga.: Wiregrass Publishing, 2008.

Hunter Jr., Malcolm L. et al. *Saving the Earth as a Career: Advice on Becoming a Conservation Professional.* Hoboken, N.J.: Wiley-Blackwell, 2007.

Jacoby, Karl. *Crimes Against Nature: Squatters, Poachers, Thieves, and the Hidden History of American Conservation.* Berkeley, Calif.: University of California Press, 2003.

Leopold, Aldo. *A Sand County Almanac (Outdoor Essays & Reflections).* New York: Oxford University Press, 2001.

Luttrell, Jean. *John H. Riffey: The Last Old-Time Ranger.* Flagstaff, Ariz.: Vishnu Temple Press, 2007.

McMahon, Robert. *The Environmental Protection Agency: Structuring Motivation In A Green Bureaucracy, The Conflict Between Regulatory Style And Cultural Identity.* East Sussex, England: Sussex Academic Press, 2006.

Mintz, Joel A. *Enforcement at the EPA: High Stakes and Hard Choices.* Austin, Texas: University of Texas Press, 1995.

Moeller, Dade W. *Environmental Health: Third Edition.* Cambridge, Mass.: Harvard University Press, 2004.

Muir, John, and Edwin Way Teale, ed. *The Wilderness World of John Muir.* New York: Mariner Books, 2001.

Muleady-Mecham, Nancy Eileen. *Park Ranger: True Stories from a Ranger's Career in America's National Parks.* Flagstaff, Ariz.: Vishnu Temple Press, 2004.

Muleady-Mecham, Nancy Eileen. *Park Ranger Sequel.* Flagstaff, Ariz.: Vishnu Temple Press, 2008.

Novick, Lloyd F. *Public Health: Administration Principles for Population-based Management.* Sudbury, Mass.: Jones and Bartlett Publishers, 2007.

Pinchot, Gifford. *The Fight for Conservation.* Teddington, England: Echo Library, 2008.

Pitman, Dick. *A Wild Life: Adventures of an Accidental Conservationist in Africa.* Guilford, Conn.: The Lyons Press, 2008.

Powell, Orville W. *City Management: Keys to Success.* Bloomington, Ind.: AuthorHouse, 2002.

Rudman, Jack. *Environmental Conservation Officer Trainee (Career Examination Series).* Syosset, N.Y.: Natural Learning Corporation, 2006.

Steen, Harold. *The Conservation Diaries of Gifford Pinchot.* Durham, N.C.: Forest History Society, 2001.

Toulmin, Harry Aubrey. *The City Manager: A New Profession.* Dearborn, Mich.: University of Michigan Library, 2009.

Vig, Norman J. and Michael K. Kraft. *Environmental Policy: New Directions for the Twenty-first Century.* Washington, D.C.: CQ Press, 2009.

Worster, Donald. *A Passion for Nature: The Life of John Muir.* New York: Oxford University Press, 2008.

Index